CENSUS OF INDIA 1921

VOLUME II

THE ANDAMAN

AND

NICOBAR ISLANDS

PART I—REPORT

PART II—TABLES

The publication of decenniai census reports was initiated by the British Government during the middle of the nineteenth century and has been continued after independence. Questions of reliability and bias in the compilation of information as well as motivations which informed the publication of these reports have been raised and are relevant to every user of census reports. Even so, the censuses were often conducted with painstaking efforts and have preserved for us extremely wide-ranging information on the social, economic and political aspects of Indian life.

They contain information on the distribution and age structure of the population; castes and communities, patterns of occupation, patterns of land-holding and tenancy, health, migration, language, and education, etc., to name just a few aspects of the panorama of India society. For researchers interested in understanding Indian life, the reports of the decennial census complied by British officers remain, despite the problems of bias, misunderstanding or conscious distortion, an invaluable source of information.

The census reports consisted of two parts: a general social and economic profile and statistical material. The general profile contains an account of the census operations, the geographical and physical features of the area, the ethnography of caste and communities and changes in age-structure, health, education, employment, landholding pattern and tenancy, etc. The statistical part contains data on geography, rainfall, temperature, distribution of population according to different demographic criteria, caste and communities, health, education, employment and migration, and landholding and tenancy.

Census reports have, as a rule, been used by demographers, economists and economic historians, and a great deal of this use has been limited to the statistical data contained in them. Sociologists, social historians and political scientists have made very little use of these reports. These reports provide, particularly in the volumes entitled 'General Reports' which were published separately for each state as well as for India as a whole, ethnographic information on castes and tribes, describing their internal organization, social changes taking place in them, and the emerging problems of interaction among the different castes and communities. Social movements and trends towards social mobility among the castes and communities are also often discussed. Even from the viewpoint of the sociologists and social historians, therefore, the census reports are invaluable sources of information and can provide useful material on how the different sections of Indian society were responding to the processes set in motion by British rule.

The census reports are today a body of rare documents available in only a few select libraries and even these libraries do not always have all the available volumes which in an average census year extended to more than a hundred for the whole of India. This reprint of Parts I and II of Census of India 1921 for the Andaman and Nicobar Islands is published in the hope that it will be welcomed by individual researchers as well as libraries.

CENSUS OF INDIA 1921

VOLUME II

THE ANDAMAN
AND
NICOBAR ISLANDS

PART I – REPORT

PART II – TABLES

BY

R.F. LOWIS

Superintendent of Census Operations

MANOHAR

2001

Rs 750

First published 1923
Reprinted 2001

ISBN 81-7304-388-4

Published by
Ajay Kumar Jain for
Manohar Publishers & Distributors
4753/23 Ansari Road, Daryaganj
New Delhi 110 002

Printed at
Mehra Offset Press
1979, Ganj Mirkhan
Chandni Mahal, Daryaganj
New Delhi 110002

CENSUS OF INDIA 1921

VOLUME II

THE ANDAMAN
AND
NICOBAR ISLANDS

Part I—REPORT

Part II—TABLES

BY

R. F. LOWIS,

Superintendent of Census Operations

CALCUTTA
SUPERINTENDENT GOVERNMENT PRINTING, INDIA
1923

[Price Rs. 5 or English 6*s*. 8*d*.]

Agents for the Sale of Books published by the Superintendent of Government Printing India, Calcutta.

IN EUROPE.

Constable & Co., 10, Orange Street, Leicester Square, London, W.C.

Kegan Paul, Trench, Trübner & Co., 68-74, Carter Lane, E.C., and 39, New Oxford Street, London, W.C.

Bernard Quaritch, 11, Grafton Street, New Bond Street, London, W.

P. S. King & Sons, 2 & 4, Great Smith Street, Westminster, London, S.W.

H. S. King & Co., 65, Cornhill, E.C., and 9, Pall Mall, London, W.

Grindlay & Co., 54, Parliament Street, London, S.W.

Luzac & Co., 46, Great Russell Street, London, W.C.

W. Thacker & Co., 2, Creed Lane, London, E.C.

T. Fisher Unwin, Ltd., 1, Adelphi Terrace, London, W.C.

Wheldon and Wesley Ltd., 2, 3 & 4, Arthur Street, New Oxford Street, London, W.C. 2.

B. H. Blackwell, 50 & 51, Broad Street, Oxford.

Deighton Bell & Co., Ltd., Cambridge.

Oliver and Boyd, Tweeddale Court, Edinburgh.

E. Ponsonby, Ltd., 116, Grafton Street, Dublin.

Ernest Leroux, 28, Rue Bonaparte, Paris.

Martinus Nijhoff, The Hague, Holland.

Otto Harrassowitz, Leipzig.

Friedländer and Sohn, Berlin.

IN INDIA AND CEYLON.

Thacker, Spink & Co., Calcutta and Simla.

Newman & Co., Ltd., Calcutta.

R. Cambray & Co., Calcutta.

S. K. Lahiri & Co., Calcutta.

B. Banerjee & Co., Calcutta.

The Indian School Supply Depôt, 309, Bow Bazar Street, Calcutta, and 226, Nawabpur, Dacca.

Butterworth & Co. (India), Ltd., Calcutta.

Rai M. C. Sarcar Bahadur & Sons, 90-2A, Harrison Road, Calcutta.

The Weldon Library, 57, Park Street, West, Calcutta.

Standard Literature Co., Ltd., Calcutta.

Lal Chand & Sons, Calcutta.

Association Press, Calcutta.

The International Budhist Book Depôt, 4, Chandney Chowk, 1st Lane, Calcutta.

Higginbotham & Co., Madras.

V. Kalyanarama Iyer & Co., Madras.

G. A. Natesan & Co., Madras.

S. Murthy & Co., Madras.

Thompson & Co., Madras.

Temple & Co., Madras.

P. R. Rama Iyer & Co., Madras.

Vas & Co., Madras.

E. M. Gopalakrishna Kone, Madura.

Thacker & Co., Ltd., Bombay.

D. B. Taraporevala, Sons & Co., Bombay.

Mrs. Radhabai Atmaram Sagoon, Bombay.

Sunder Pandurang, Bombay.

Gopal Narayan & Co., Bombay.

Ram Chandra Govind & Son, Kalbadevi, Bombay.

Proprietor, New Kitabkhana, Poona.

The Standard Bookstall, Karachi.

Mangaldas Harkisandas, Surat.

Karsandas Narandas & Sons, Surat.

A. H. Wheeler & Co., Allahabad, Calcutta and Bombay.

N. B. Mathur, Supt., Nazir Kanun Hind Press, Allahabad.

Munshi Seetaram, Managing Proprietor, Indian Army Book Depôt, Juhi, Cawnpore.

Rai Sahib M. Gulab Singh & Sons, Mufid-i-Am Press, Lahore and Allahabad.

Rama Krishna & Sons, Lahore.

Supt., American Baptist Mission Press, Rangoon.

Proprietor, Rangoon Times Press, Rangoon.

The Modern Publishing House, Ltd., 70, Sparks Street, Rangoon.

Manager, the "Hitavada," Nagpur.

S. C. Talukdar, Proprietor, Students & Co., Cooch Behar.

A. M. & J. Ferguson, Ceylon.

Manager, Educational Book Depôts, Nagpur and Jubbulpore.*

Manager of the Imperial Book Depôt, 63, Chandney Chauk Street, Delhi.*

Manager, "The Agra Medical Hall and Co-operative Association, Ltd." (Successors to A. John & Co., Agra.)*

Supt., Basel Mission Book and Tract Depository, Mangalore.*

P. Varadachary & Co., Madras.*

Ram Dayal Agarwala, 184, Katra, Allahabad.*

D. C. Anand & Sons, Peshawar.*

Manager, Newal Kishore Press, Lucknow.*

Maung Lu Gale, Proprietor, Law Book Depôt, Mandalay.*

Times of Ceylon Co., Ltd.†

Agents for the sale of Legislative Department publications only.
† Agents for the sale of Archæological publications only.

TABLE OF CONTENTS.

PART I—REPORT.

APPENDICES.

PART II.—TABLES.

INTRODUCTION.

IN this Report I propose to deal very briefly with the results of the Census of the Andamans and Nicobars for 1921. For various reasons, on which I need not dilate, it is impossible for me to devote to the work the time necessary to produce a report on even the restricted lines of that of 1911. At the same time the threads of the work have been so much in my own hands, and the subjects dealt with are of such a nature, that it would be difficult for my successor, or in fact, anyone now in the Settlement, to deal adequately with the subject.

The figures, or those for the Settlement at any rate, are of no scientific interest. The Settlement is a purely artificial institution, and tables, and statistics relating principally to convicts are of little or no value. The story of the industrial development of India is not affected by our returns; all available matter of ethnological interest has already been given in previous reports: and so it seemed to me questionable whether in the circumstances any report to accompany the Tables was necessary. The Census Commissioner, when the matter was referred to him on the occasion of his visiting the Settlement, was of opinion that something to carry on and bring up to date the information given in the last Census Report, particularly in regard to the indigenous populations, their distribution, movement &c., was desirable; and he suggested that I should leave some notes on these subjects for publication with the Tables. This I propose to do on the strength of the provisional totals, as I will have left India before the tabulation of the figures is complete. The numbers dealt with are so small that any difference that there may be between the provisional and final totals will not be sufficiently great to affect the conclusions arrived at.

I propose to limit the Report to two chapters. The first dealing with the Census will form with the diaries &c. in the Appendices something in the nature of an Administrative Volume. The second will deal with the distribution and movement of the various communities dealt with.

I regret that I have not more information of ethnological interest to include in this Report. The Reports of 1901 and 1911 contain practically all that is available of a general nature. Any notes which I consider to be of sufficient interest for publication will be found in the form of appendices.

I am including an account of an interesting ceremony witnessed by the Rev. W. R. Park, C.I.E. at Lapati village on Car Nicobar in March 1915, which account I obtained from him at the time. My acknowledgments are due to him on publication of the same.

I am also indebted to the Rev. G. Whitehead, at one time in charge of the S. P. G. Mission on Car Nicobar, and to Mr. E. Hart, Government Agent on the Island for certain folk-lore stories, and notes on the religious observances of the Nicobarese.

Owing to my absence on tour during the month preceding the taking of the Census I was compelled to leave entirely in the hands of Mr. Bunyad Hussain, B. A., Revenue Assistant Commissioner, and District Census Officer all arrangements for the taking of the Census in the Settlement. In doing this I was confident that the work would be well done, and the results prove, I think, that my confidence was not misplaced.

I would take this opportunity to express my gratitude to all those persons on whom responsibility was thrown in connection with the taking of the Census; more particularly to Messrs. Bonington, D. C. Forests, and O'Hara, E. A. C. Forests, who arranged for the taking of the Census in the forest camps under their charge; and also to Mr. E. Hart, and to Babu Mewa Lall, Assistant Government Agent, Nancowry for the enumeration of the Nicobarese. My thanks are also due to Mr. R. Wilkinson, Assistant Commissioner, Port Blair, who accompanied me to the Nicobars, and assisted me in the enumeration of the outlying Islands.

Lastly, I would wish to express my appreciation of the services of Captain Glanville, R. I. M. and Officers R. I. M. S. Minto on whom devolved the responsibility of taking the Census party round the Nicobars. Those who are acquainted with these seas will appreciate the trouble and responsibility involved in the navigation of even a small vessel like the Minto, under highly unpropitious weather conditions, in the dangerous and practically unsurveyed waters of these Islands.

PORT BLAIR: R. F. LOWIS,
15th April, 1921. *Supdt., Census Operations.*

CENSUS OF INDIA

1921

REPORT

ON THE

ANDAMANS AND NICOBARS.

CHAPTER I.

The Census.

I. General.

For the Census of 1921 the Administration was divided, as on the occasion of the last Census, into three sections:

1. The Settlement of Port Blair.
2. The Andamanese.
3. The Nicobars.

The method of taking the Census differed in the case of each unit. In the Settlement of Port Blair the Census was synchronous, and carried out in accordance with the procedure laid down in the Imperial Census Code. In the case of the Andamanese a synchronous Census was not possible. It was arranged that the friendly tribes in Great Andaman should be numbered by direct enumeration; the Superintendent, Census Operations, himself making a tour round the Islands for the purpose. In the case of the Önges on Rutland and Little Andaman, these Islands were visited also by the Superintendent, Census Operations, in the course of his tours, and an effort was made to get in touch with as many of the aboriginals as was possible, and an estimate of their numbers was formed on the strength of the information gained. The Jarawas in South Andaman and North Sentinel being uniformly hostile no attempt was made at direct enumeration, and their numbers were estimated on the information obtained in the course of the various expeditions organized against the tribe. The Census of the Nicobars was non-synchronous, the enumeration being done on standard forms by the Agent and Assistant Agent during February. The Superintendent, Census Operations visited the Islands in March, and took the Census on those Islands to which the Agents had not easy access.

II. Census of the Settlement.

The problem of organizing the Census of the Settlement of Port Blair presented no difficulties. The population is, in a sense, homogeneous, and easily accessible. As regards the convicts, who form the bulk of the population, records exist rendering the process of enumeration almost unnecessary. On this occasion we had the experience of 1911 to guide us, and the scheme then evolved was adopted with a few minor alterations.

The services of a whole-time officer could not be spared as in the case of the 1911 Census, and it became necessary to decentralize authority and responsibility as far as possible. The Deputy Commissioner was appointed Superintendent of Operations, and the Revenue Assistant Commissioner was made District Census Officer, and the operations in the Settlement were carried out by him under the general orders of the Superintendent of Operations.

Copies of all orders, and the District Census Officer's Report showing how these were carried out, will be found in an Appendix to the Report, taking the place of a separate Administrative Volume.

Generally speaking, the scheme worked smoothly throughout, and without any serious hitch; at the same time there are one or two points with regard to which improvement might be effected.

In house numbering, all buildings, whether residential or not, were included in the house lists. This entailed much extra work, not only in the operations outside, but also in the preparation of the schedules; and when these were completed it was not easy to check the entries with the house lists.

In defining the duties of the District Census Officer the Superintendent of Operations himself assumed responsibility for the Census of Military units in direct communication with the Officers commanding the same; and also for the Census of the Forest Camps outside the confines of the Settlement; the work of enumeration in these camps being carried out through the agency of the resident Forest Officers.

Now in Port Blair the troops are not, as is generally the case in India, located in clearly defined cantonments, and experience on this occasion proved that it would have been better if the District Census Officer had been made responsible for the Census of Military units, as this would have minimized the chances of omission or double enumeration.

As regards the Census of the Forest Camps there were not the same chances of overlapping, and it was certainly easier for the Superintendent of Operations himself to control this branch of the work rather than the District Census Officer whose ordinary duties do not take him outside the limits of the Settlement.

III. Census of the Andamanese.

A synchronous census of the Andamanese was not possible; in fact, it was only possible to obtain the numbers of a small proportion of the race by direct enumeration. In the case of the Yerewa and Bojigngiji groups, the friendly tribes in Great Andaman, direct enumeration was possible.

In the case of the Önges it was possible to obtain exact figures with regard to only one section of the tribe, and for the rest estimate had to be resorted to.

In the case of the Jarawas estimate alone was possible.

(a) The Yerewa and Bojigngiji.

As indicated above the enumeration of these groups presented no great difficulties. As the result of contact with civilization they are so reduced in numbers that it is fairly easy to locate all parties and camps; each member of these groups is well known to all the rest; from November to April the majority are concentrated in the camps established for the collection of the various natural products of the Islands, such as resin, tortoise-shell, trepang, mother-of-pearl and the like, which are sold for the benefit of the Andaman Homes: it is therefore possible to arrive at their numbers with a degree of accuracy impossible in the case of the other tribes.

It was not of course possible to see each man and woman enumerated. There are generally some hunting parties separate from the main camps which cannot be quickly located, though often they can be called in in a few hours; occasionally, as happened this time in the case of parties out in the Stewart Sound Basin, their whereabouts is not known, and details with regard to their numbers &c., have to be obtained indirectly. Given time it is possible to get in touch with all, but my time was very restricted, and I did not consider that I was justified in delaying my tour when I was confident that the information I was able to obtain of the numbers and composition of the absent parties was, to all intents and purposes, exact, sufficiently so in any case to form a correct estimate of the movement of this section of the population.

(b) The Önges.

The taking of the Census of the Önges was not so simple. Except in the case of the Septs located on Rutland, and in the north of Little Andaman, who have been in fairly continuous touch with civilization, direct enumeration of only a very small percentage of the tribe was possible. The attitude of the other Septs towards strangers is still a little uncertain. At the time of the last Census Messrs. Bonig and Fawcett toured the Island and were received everywhere without a trace of hostility.

The Island has not been visited from the Settlement since 1911, and the only contact between the Önges of the south and the outside world occurred some three years ago when a Chinese junk, trading between Penang and the Nicobars was blown out of its course and fetched up at Little Andaman. There according to the Chinese they were wantonly attacked by the aboriginals. That they were attacked there is little doubt as they brought away a number of arrows fired into the ship, one of which wounded the Master in the neck; but whether the attack was really unprovoked, and by which Sept it was carried out it is impossible to prove.

Whether the Önges have lapsed during the past ten years into some of their old bad habits is not quite clear. We encountered no hostility; but we saw only very few of the inhabitants, very many fewer than were seen by Messrs. Bonig and Fawcett in 1911. This may have been pure chance; for of the empty huts we saw, only one showed signs of occupation at the time of the visit. It is true that one party seen on the beach retired into the jungle on the approach of the boat, and refused to come out; but under the circumstances a certain amount of shyness was to be expected. Whether therefore our lack of success was chance or design I cannot say. It is certain, however, that those Önges with whom we came in contact were perfectly friendly, and not in the least timid.

Including the Sept or Septs enumerated in Rutland we saw only 99 Önges in the course of our trip:—

Place.	Men.	Women.	Boys.	Girls.	Total.
Tochiewe	6	..	1	..	7
Toibalawe	6	5	3	2	16
Toreada	5	3	5	2	15
Rutland	27	18	8	8	61
Total	44	26	17	12	99

It is difficult on this slender basis to estimate the number of the whole tribe.

The greatest disability we laboured under was lack of time. In order to arrive at a correct idea of the population it is essential to spend on the Island a very much longer period than was possible in our case. I should say that not less than a month would be necessary to gain the complete confidence of the natives; nor would this I believe be difficult, or attended with great risk or inconvenience.

As the result of my observations on the occasion of my visit I formed the opinion that the numbers of the Önges in the Census of 1911 were placed much too high. On that occasion 286 Önges were actually seen, *viz*:—118 men, 78 women, 62 boys, 28 girls.

In estimating the population it was assumed that two-thirds of the men had been seen, and it was also assumed that the number of men seen approximated more closely to actuals than in the case of women and children, because it was thought probable that some of the latter were purposely kept out of sight. Having arrived at the supposed number of men, women were allowed for in the proportion found among the friendly tribes on Great Andaman, and children were allowed for on a very liberal scale.

As the result of my observations this year I am convinced that my assumptions in 1911 were wrong. It is probably true that on that occasion the whole tribe was not seen; but I believe that those seen were in the correct proportion as to sexes, adults, and children. In the case of those parties seen by us this year males predominated over females in a very marked degree, and the proportion of the sexes in the south was about the same as that found in the case of the Önge inhabitants of Rutland, for whom we have exact figures; moreover these proportions are very nearly the same as those observed among the Önges actually seen in 1911.

If we assume that the number of men estimated in 1911 was correct and add women and children in the proportion found this year we arrive at an estimated population for 1911 of:—

Men 177, women 121, boys 75, girls 56, or a total population of 429.

If on the other hand we assume that the number actually seen in 1911 was two-thirds of the whole population, we arrive at exactly the same total, *i.e.*, 286 *plus* 143 equals 429.

I believe this estimate to be much nearer the truth than the one given in the Census Report of 1911.

The next question is whether these figures correctly represent the present population, or whether there has been movement upwards or downwards in the last decade. The evidence on which any estimate must perforce be based is very inexact, and my figures are, I admit, subject to criticism.

What evidence there is tends to show that the population is decreasing. Mr. Bonig at the time of the last Census gave it as his opinion, based on observations extending over several years, that the Önges were decreasing in numbers; and all evidence collected at the present Census tends to confirm this view.

As to the degree of decrease the evidence is very inexact. It is of course, impossible to base any estimate on the number of Önges seen this year as compared with the number seen in 1911. The only points for comparison are:—

(1) The number of communal huts seen this year as compared with the number seen by the 1911 party.

(2) The number of Önges enumerated this year on Rutland as compared with the number found there in 1911.

Taking first the number of huts. We found 14 as compared with 19 in the 1911 Census; that is to say, a decrease of about 26 %.

As regards the number of Önges on Rutland. In 1911 there were (according to Mr. Bonig's diary of the tour) about 80 on the Island; whereas on the present occasion we enumerated 61 on Rutland; a decrease of 25 %.

If we assume that the correct number of the whole tribe in 1911 was as now estimated by me 429, and allow for a decrease of 25 % in the last decade we arrive at a present population of 344.

If I were called upon to make an independent estimate of the number of the Önges now in Little Andaman I would base it on the number of communal huts observed in the course of our tour round the Island. It seems to me that the Önges are divided into clearly defined Septs, and that these Septs have little or no communication with one another. Mr. Bonig as the result of his observations at the last Census came to the conclusion that this was not the case; but the proofs we obtained of these well-defined divisions were fairly clear. The Önges we brought with us from Rutland to help us to get in touch with those in Little Andaman gave us information, (not always I admit correct), with regard to communities in the neighbourhood of Bumila Creek, and the north end of the Island, and as far south as Jackson Creek; but beyond this point they expressed complete ignorance of the location or number of huts. They explained that the country beyond this point was outside their sphere, and that if they trespassed there they ran the risk of being shot. We had the same experience with two men we took on board near Tochiewe. These belonged to a different Sept to the Rutland men; they were able to assist us with regard to a further stretch of coast; but having arrived at the limit of their beat they expressed ignorance of the adjoining terrain in nearly the same terms as the Rutland men had done.

That the tribe is divided into Septs seems to me clear, and it is equally clear that each Sept is subdivided into small communal parties occupying one communal hut. The communal huts we saw were all situated on the shore, and visible from the sea; they were of uniform shape and size, and judging by the sleeping accommodation were designed for the occupation of approximately the same number of persons. That these communal huts are not in permanent occupation we had proof, but none were permanently abandoned so far as we could judge, and I believe that each hut represents one communal party. We have of course, no proof that each communal party on the Island has a hut on the coast; in fact, I think, this is unlikely; but in view of the wide separation of the coast huts, and the large area over which the Andamanese has to roam to get a living by hunting and fishing alone it seems likely that those in the interior are less numerous than those on the coast.

As regards the average number in one communal unit the data is not very extensive. We actually saw two such units, and the men belonging to two more, and from the information gleaned from them I believe that the parties we saw were average units and that the number per unit may be put down at 15.

We saw 14 huts on the Island, and if we assume that this was two-thirds of the number on the Island we arrive at a total population of 376, or 30 more than by assuming a reduction of 25 % on the estimated figures of last Census. It is impossible to say which estimate is the most correct, or whether either is anywhere near the truth. Possibly the estimate of huts in the interior is rather high. If we allow for 19 huts in all the estimates about coincide.

I therefore estimate the Önge tribe as below :—

Men 144, women 100, boys 60, girls 42, total 346.

(c) The Jarawas.

Any attempt at direct enumeration in the case of the Jarawas was impossible. This tribe has been consistently hostile ever since the establishment of the Settlement. All attempts to enter into friendly relations with them have failed. As long as they confined their activities to attacking only parties who invaded that section of the country which is recognised as their particular zone they could hardly be blamed. Just about the time of the last Census however, they developed a tendency to leave their own jungles and attack settlers in the fields, and on the roads on the outskirts of the Settlement, and it became necessary to take measures to check these tendencies.

The first punitive expedition in 1910, of which an account appeared in the last Census Report, seemed to have the desired effect, in spite of the fact that very little harm was done to the Jarawas; at any rate their activities were restricted for some time to their own territories. In 1917 however, a number of very daring raids took place, in one of which a train on the Gopalakabang steam tram line was held up.

The punitive expedition undertaken in the spring of 1918 was not an unqualified success, and the effect did not last long, and by the winter of 1920 the Jarawas were as active as ever. On one occasion they attacked a camp of convicts employed on collecting canes in a part of the country which had always been looked upon as well outside the territorial limits of the tribe. On this occasion they killed no less than five men, and wounded three others.

Another punitive expedition was organized in the spring of this year; but no tangible results were achieved, and it is not likely to have a strong deterrent effect.

It is on the information obtained on these expeditions that the numbers of the tribe in South Andaman is based. I am publishing with this Report some extracts from diaries of the last two expeditions , a perusal of which will show that they do not throw much light on the question of the movement of the population; so in the absence of any grounds for amending the estimate arrived at at the last Census, I adhere to it for the Census of 1921.

As regards the Jarawas on North Sentinel, the Island has not been visited during the last decade, and there are no grounds for supposing that there have been any alterations in the conditions prevailing there which would affect the numbers, and here again I adhere to the estimate arrived at in 1911.

IV. The Census of the Nicobars.

As already stated a synchronous Census of the Nicobars was not, in existing circumstances, possible. It was arranged, however, to enumerate the population (exclusive of the wild Shom Pen tribe in the interior of Great Nicobar) on the standard schedules in the same way as was done last year.

The Census on the majority of the Islands was taken during February and the first week of March by the Government Agent at Car Nicobar, and by the

Assistant Agent in the Central Group, whilst I proceeded myself on tour round the Islands between the 5th and the 15th March, and took the Census on those Islands to which the Agents have not easy access.

Owing tc the somewhat late receipt of the supply of schedule forms these were only issued to the Agents on the 12th and 13th of February respectively. This only left them about three weeks in which to make the enumeration, and fill up the forms, which in the case of the Agent at Car Nicobar who had a population of over six thousand to deal with, was hardly enough. The Assistant Agent at Nancowry, although he had very many fewer persons to enumerate, had to travel over a considerable area in connection with the work ; however, both were in the end able to complete the work, and hand in their schedules on the prescribed date.

The arrangements generally were the same as last year ; but owing to the greater facilities enjoyed by the Assistant Agent for moving about between Islands I extended the scope of his operations somewhat, and made him responsible for the Census of the Islands of Teressa and Bompoka in addition to the Central Group. It remained, therefore, for me only to carry out the enumeration of Chaura, and of the islands of the Southern Group on the occasion of my tour in March.

I left Port Blair in R. I. M. S. Minto on the 6th March, accompanied by Mr. Wilkinson, A. C. Port Blair. The programme laid down was carried out without any serious hitch. The weather was not over propitious which added to the difficulty of the operation, and in the course of the enumeration of villages on Great Nicobar the Census party was very nearly involved in disaster. The work was however, carried to a successful conclusion, and I believe that the results obtained are as exact as those of the previous Census.

The Shom Pen.

I have not been able to collect very much information regarding the location or numbers of this tribe since the last Census. The Nicobarese still appear to live in dread of them, and speak as if an attack by them was imminent, although, so far as I have been able to ascertain, there has been no Shom Pen raid for over 20 years ; at the same time the concentration of all Nicobarese at Pulo Babi and on Megapod Island is certainly attributable to their fear of the Shom Pen.

I asked the Head-man at Pulo Babi if he had any idea how many Shom Pen there were in the interior. He replied that there were about 100 in that neighbourhood ; but he could not say what proportion this is of the whole tribe.

That there are Shom Pen in other parts of the Island I had proof when I visited Galatea Bay in the Sunbeam in 1918 for I came across a recently abandoned encampment in the jungle about half a mile from the shore ; but where else they are to be found, and how many there are it is impossible to say.

I had hoped to arrange for a boat trip up the Galatea River on the 13th March, on the chance of coming across Shom Pen, but the state of the weather, and the consequent surf on the bar at the mouth of the river made the trip impossible.

In the absence of any information showing that my estimate of the numbers of the Shom Pen in 1911 was wrong, or that there has been any subsequent movement in the population I adhere to these figures for the present Census.

V. The Industrial Census of Port Blair.

An industrial Census on the lines laid down for the rest of India was not taken in the Settlement, where conditions are not the same as in other parts of the Empire and where private enterprise is not encouraged. I have, however, prepared a statement giving the various industrial units in the Settlement, and the labour employed in each ; from this may be deduced the number of skilled workmen, and the industrial development of the place.

Port Blair Industrial Census.

INDUSTRIAL UNIT.	SKILLED LABOUR.																									SPECIALIZED LABOUR.										UN-SKILLED LABOUR.	
	Supervising Staff.	Foremen.	Carpenters.	Turners, coopers, wheel-wrights and coach builders.	Sawyers.	Carvers.	Caulkers.	Blacksmiths.	Tinsmiths.	Boilermakers, platers and rivetters.	Brass and Copper workers.	Watchmakers and Silversmiths.	Engine drivers.	Fitters.	Machine men.	Workers in cane.	Net makers.	Weavers.	Tailors.	Workers in mother-of-pearl and tortoise-shell.	Shoemakers.	Brick masons.	Stone masons.	Typesetters and printers.	Book binders.	Fibre extractors.	Rope makers.	Thatchers.	Warp makers.	Quarry men.	Brick moulders and burners.	Coke makers.	Charcoal burners.	Cocoanut pluckers.	Tappers of rubber.	Un-skilled labour.	TOTAL.
Public Works Department	4	30	196	17	..	..	..	17	1	..	..	..	6	2	..	..	..	..	..	..	..	91	33	..	..	..	..	..	..	33	..	2	..	..	..	375	807
Government Work Shops	2	26	113	18	7	..	11	16	1	22	2	1	11	24	30	..	..	..	5	..	8	..	..	..	..	..	..	..	..	..	..	..	..	..	..	41	338
Chatham Saw Mills	2	30	3	1	24	..	..	4	..	..	..	..	4	6	..	..	..	..	..	..	..	..	..	..	..	..	..	..	..	..	..	..	2	..	..	222	298
Cellular and Female Jails	4	65	18	..	..	..	..	7	..	..	..	..	..	..	..	46	2	97	17	..	..	..	..	25	7	162	97	..	40	..	..	..	..	..	..	124	711
Private Work Shops	1	10	22	11	..	10	..	3	1	..	9	6	..	..	..	..	..	..	1	31	6	..	..	..	..	..	..	..	..	..	..	..	..	..	..	..	111
Brickfields	1	16	4	..	3	..	..	3	..	..	..	..	..	3	..	2	..	..	..	..	..	..	..	..	..	..	..	9	..	..	48	..	8	..	..	156	253
Cocoanut Plantations	4	10	..	..	..	..	..	..	..	..	..	..	..	..	..	..	..	..	..	..	..	..	..	..	..	..	..	..	..	..	..	..	..	102	..	84	200
Rubber Plantation	2	14	..	..	..	..	..	..	..	..	..	..	..	..	..	..	..	..	..	..	..	..	..	..	..	..	..	..	..	..	..	..	..	..	14	75	105
Coffee Plantation	1	11	..	..	..	..	..	..	..	..	..	..	..	..	..	..	..	..	..	..	..	..	..	..	..	..	..	..	..	..	..	..	..	..	..	13	15
TOTAL	21	202	356	47	34	10	11	50	3	22	11	7	21	35	30	48	2	97	23	31	14	91	33	25	7	162	97	9	40	33	48	2	10	102	14	1,090	2,838

NOTE.—In this statement male and female workers are not shown separately. In case separate figures are required the details for female workers are given here

Skilled	Net makers	2
	Weavers	82
	Tailors	10
Specialized	Warp makers	40

I have not included the operations of the Forest Department in my statement; but timber will probably always be the principal industry in the Andamans; nevertheless the Islands lend themselves to agricultural development, and to the production of raw materials on a considerable scale; and with the closing of the Penal Settlement, and the free admission of private enterprise, it is possible that there may be progress in this direction in the near future.

The soil and climate of the Andamans are admirably suited for the production of cocoanuts, rubber, Liberian Coffee, Sisal hemp, Manilla hemp, Sea Island cotton, and sugar-cane, all of which have been experimented with. There are already over 2,000 acres of cocoanut plantation in being, which bring in to Government a considerable revenue; also 600 acres of rubber is just coming into bearing which is already yielding an appreciable cash return; besides the above a small plantation of 144 acres of Liberian Coffee is leased to a contractor, who pays Government a yearly rent of Rs. 2,000 for the same. Sisal hemp, Manilla hemp, and sugar-cane are at present only grown to supply local requirements, but are capable of almost unlimited development. The growing of cotton is still hardly beyond the experimental stage, but the crop promises extremely well.

It will be seen from the above that the Statement which is attached herewith in no way represents the industrial possibilities of the Andaman Islands.

CHAPTER II.

Distribution and Movement.

I. General.

Table showing movement of population, and distribution.

Year.	Settlement.			Andamanese.			Nicobars.			Total.		
	M.	F.	Total.	M.	F	Total	M.	F.	Total.	M.	F.	Total.
1911 . . .	14,109	2,215	16,324	628	689	1,317	4,833	3,985	8,818	19,570	6,889	26,459
1921 . . .	15,221	2,047	17.268	414	372	786	5,238	4,022	9,260	20,873	6,441	27,314

The above figures show the distribution of the population and the numbers as they stood in 1911, and in 1921. This table indicates a slight upward movement, but the conditions obtaining in the three sections into which the population is divided are so diverse that it is waste of time to consider the returns as a whole; the questions of distribution and movement will be considered separately in reference to the figures of each section.

II. The Settlement.

(A) Distribution. The Penal Settlement of Port Blair is situated in South Andaman on the harbour of that name.

The first attempt to colonise these Islands was made in the year 1789 when a colony was established on this same harbour by Captain Archibald Blair, R.N. This colony or Settlement was later moved to what is now known as Port Cornwallis in North Andaman, the idea being that it would eventually become a naval base. This scheme did not, however, mature, and after a chequered career covering only seven years the colony was closed in the year 1796.

The question of establishing a colony in the Andamans as a place of refuge for the crews of ships wrecked onthe coasts was again mooted some sixty years later; but the present Penal Settlement was actually opened in the year 1858 for the accommodation of the vast numbers of prisoners resulting from the quelling of the mutiny, for whom accommodation could not be found in India.

The Settlement has developed and expanded considerably since those early days. It now covers an area of something like 330 square miles of arable and grazing land, interspersed with forest. The population still consists principally of convicts, there being in the Settlement at the time of the Census 11,555 convicts as against 4,132 free persons, *i.e.*, officials, garrison, police, and free settlers; one free person to every two convicts.

The above figures do not include the population of the Forest Camps, which are, strictly speaking, not part of the Settlement.

The forests of the Andamans, which are of great economic value, were exploited by the Imperial Forest Department for many years with convict labour. In time, however, the forests in the immediate vicinity of the Settlement were worked out, and the Department were obliged to extend their operations further afield, where convict labour could not be employed.

There are at present two Forest centres in the Andamans, separate from the Settlement, but controlled from it. One of these is in Middle Andaman, and the other in Stewart Sound in North Andaman. These camps are populated principally by coolies imported from India, a very large proportion of whom return to India after working some six months in the Islands. The number of persons enumerated in these camps at the time of the Census was 1,581, of whom 1,511 were males, and 70 females.

For purposes of tabulation the population of the Forest Camps has been included in the Settlement.

The figures for the Settlement may be conveniently subdivided into communities as below:—

Officials and Free Residents born outside the Settlement	651
Garrison and Military Police Battalions	978
Locally born Free and Ex-Convict population	2,503
Convicts	11,555
Total Population in Settlement	15,687
Population in Forest Camps	1,581
Total Population in Tables	17,268

(B) Movement.

Year.	Settlement.		
	M.	F.	Total.
1911	14,109	2,215	16,324
1921	15,221	2,047	17,268

The population of the Settlement is built up on a purely artificial basis; the forces which operate to cause an increase or a decrease in the numbers are not natural or even economic but purely administrative. The movement of the population is determined principally by the Government's policy in regard to transportation generally, and in a lesser degree by their actions in the matter of remissions and releases.

The Census figures of 1921 for the Settlement as a whole show a slight tendency upwards, the gross increase being 944.

As a matter of fact, in the Settlement proper, as apart from the Forest camps, there has been a decline, (from 16,324 to 15,687). This decline is general, affecting all communities. The numbers of—

Free Residents and Officials has decreased by	120
Police and Military Units by	175
Convict establishment by	342
Total decrease	637

The inclusion in the Settlement totals of persons enumerated in the forest camps (1,581) changes the adverse balance into one in favour of the Settlement by 944.

I have had taken out for the purposes of this Census the numbers of the local indigenous population, which is made up of ex-convicts, and the offspring of convicts and ex-convicts to the third and fourth generations.

Table showing the indigenous free population.

Place.	Adults ex-convict.		Adults locally born.		Adults. born in India		Children born. locally		Children born. in India.		Total males.	Total females	Total population.
	M.	F.	M.	F.	M.	F.	M.	F.	M.	F.			
Ross District	97	63	181	191	88	60	253	224	19	22	638	560	1,198
Haddo District	165	129	301	308	22	11	327	264	..	..	815	712	1,527
TOTAL	262	192	482	499	110	71	580	488	19	22	1,453	1,272	2,725

These figures are of only local interest; but in view of the approaching abandonment of the Islands as a Penal Settlement it is this local indigenous population which will have to form the nucleus of the future Settlement under the altered conditions, and much depends on how readily they adapt themselves to the same.

What the future movement of the population of these Islands will be it is impossible to foretell with any degree of accuracy, but if the Penal Settlement is abolished it is safe to say that the population will decline rapidly in the next few years; but it is impossible to tell what population will be found here at the time of the next Census. Supposing always that the evacuation of the convict population is completed within that time, and presuming that a certain number will be permitted to remain behind; and taking for granted that the economic ventures undertaken by Government, in the way of rubber, cocoanut, and coffee plantations will be taken over and developed by private enterprise, there may still be a population of about 6,000, more or less, at the time of the next Census; but the whole question is so uncertain that it is waste of time to try and anticipate events.

III. The Andamanese.

(A) Distribution.

The Andamanese, so far as is at present known, are the remnant of a Negrito race which once occupied what is now known as the Burmese Peninsula, and probably also the Tenasserim coast, and the Malay Peninsula, and Archipelago. It is quite conceivable that what are now the Andaman Islands were at one time part of the Asiatic Continent, forming a peninsula in extension of what is now Cape Negrais, but that as the result of subsidence, either gradual, or consequent on some volcanic eruption, or other cataclysm, they were cut off from the main land, and resolved themselves into a series of islands separated from the continent of India, and from each other by wide stretches of sea.

The Negrito aboriginals on the continent of India were probably swept away many thousands of years ago by succeeding waves of emigration pouring down from China, Thibet, and India, till only those who had been cut off from the parent stock on these islands, and were thus protected by their isolated position, coupled with their hostility to all strangers, survived in their primitive condition. They remain to-day a remnant of a forgotten age; living the same life, and using the same primitive weapons as did their ancestors many thousands of years ago.

The Andamanese are so far as is at present known, divided into twelve tribes. These speak different languages, or rather well marked dialects of the same common language. These tribes at the time of our occupation inhabited different parts of the Islands each adhering to its own recognised territorial limits, and having little or no communication with each other. Not only were the tribes mutually hostile to each other, but they were uniformly hostile to all strangers landing on the Islands.

It was primarily with a view to forming on the Islands a haven of refuge for the crews of wrecked ships that Blair's original Settlement of 1789, and the later Penal Settlement of 1858, were established.

The Aborigines were at first hostile to the settlers; but as time went on friendly relations were gradually established with ten out of the twelve tribes. With one tribe only on Great Andaman have we failed to come to an understanding: the Jarawas of to-day, who occupy the forests on the northern and western outskirts of the Settlement, are to this day as fiercely hostile as were their ancestors of the eighteenth century.

With the Önges in Little Andaman, owing to their isolated position we have come less in contact, and for many years their attitude was somewhat uncertain; but on the whole they may be considered as friendly, or at any rate not actively hostile.

The Andamanese race has always been treated as divided into twelve tribes, subdivided by differences of language, customs, and the weapons used into three groups:—

Yerewa Group.	Bojigngiji Group.	Önge-Jarawa, or Outer Group.
Aka-Chariar (da)	Oko-Juwaî (da)	...
Aka-Kora (da)	Aka-Kol (da)	Önge.
Aka-Tabo (da)	Aka-Bojigyab (da)	...
Aka-Yere (da)	Aka-Balawa (da)	Jarawa.
Aka-Kede (da)	Aka-Bea (da)	...

By language, habits, customs, and the form of weapons used the Yerewa and Bojigngiji Groups are very much more closely related to each other than to the Önges or Jarawas, who in turn show much more affinity to each other than to the two northern Groups.

I think myself that a more correct classification would be into two main groups; each main group being divided into two sub-groups and each sub-group further subdivided into tribes.

So far as we are at present aware the Önges are not divided into tribes; but they are certainly divided into mutually hostile Septs, and it is quite possible that these Septs have tribal names of which we are ignorant. Tribal divisions of this nature are not always apparent at first sight. It was only after many years careful observation that the tribal divisions of the Yerewa and Bojigngiji groups were finally established, and our relations with these groups were more intimate fifty years ago than are our relations with the Önges to-day.

As regards the Jarawas we know even less than of the Önges. The name Jarawa is not the name of a tribe, it is simply the Bea word for a stranger. It is quite possible that they were at one time, and possibly still are divided into mutually hostile tribes or septs. The Andamanese on North Sentinel are classed as Jarawas; and from what is known of their general characteristics there is no doubt that they are closely allied to the Önge-Jarawa Group; but as they cannot have had any communication with their fellows on the Main Island, certainly for many years, and probably for centuries, we may, I think, take it for granted that they have no greater affinity with the Jarawas on the Main land than with the Önges on Little Andaman.

I would divide the Andamanese as below:—

Aka-Chariar Aka-Kora Aka-Tabo Aka-Yere Aka-Kede	Yerewa Group	Northern Section.
Oko-Juwai Aka-Kol Aka-Balawa Aka-Bojigyab Aka-Bea	Bojigngiji Group	
Divisions unknown	Önges	Southern Section.
Divisions unknown	Jarawas	

Enumeration Statement showing numbers and distribution of Andamanese.

Tribe.	Temple Sound.				Interview Island.				Port Cornwallis.				Stewart Sound.				Havelock Island.				Andaman Home.				South Andaman.				North Sentinel Island.				Rutland.				Little Andaman.				Total.
	Men.	Women.	Boys.	Girls.	Men.	Women.	Boys.	Girls.	Men.	Women.	Boys.	Girls.	Men.	Women.	Boys.	Girls.	Men.	Women.	Boys.	Girls.	Men.	Women.	Boys.	Girls.	Men.	Women.	Boys.	Girls.	Men.	Women.	Boys.	Girls.	Men.	Women.	Boys.	Girls.	Men.	Women.	Boys.	Girls.	
Charjar	8	2	2	..	1	1	..	..	..	..	..	..	..	..	..	..	1	..	..	..	2	..	..	..	..	..	..	..	..	..	..	..	..	..	..	..	..	..	..	..	17
Kora	11	22	7	5	..	..	..	..	1	2	..	..	..	..	..	..	..	..	..	..	..	..	..	..	..	..	..	..	..	..	..	..	..	..	..	..	..	..	..	..	48
Tabo	1	..	..	1	1	1	..	..	..	..	..	..	4	5	..	4	..	..	..	..	..	1	..	..	..	..	..	..	..	..	..	..	..	..	..	..	..	..	..	..	18
Yere	4	1	..	..	14	22	8	2	..	1	..	..	13	11	2	3	..	5	1	1	7	6	..	..	..	..	..	..	..	..	..	..	..	..	..	..	..	..	..	..	101
Kede	1	..	..	..	..	..	..	..	..	..	..	..	..	..	..	..	1	3	..	..	1	..	..	..	..	..	..	..	..	..	..	..	..	..	..	..	..	..	..	..	6
Juwal	..	..	..	..	1	1	..	..	..	..	..	..	..	..	..	..	1	2	..	..	..	..	..	..	..	..	..	..	..	..	..	..	..	..	..	..	..	..	..	..	5
Kol	..	..	..	..	..	..	..	..	..	..	..	..	..	..	..	..	..	..	..	..	..	..	..	..	..	..	..	..	..	..	..	..	..	..	..	..	..	..	..	..	..
Bojigyab	..	..	..	..	..	..	..	..	..	..	..	..	..	..	..	..	6	2	..	1	..	..	..	..	..	..	..	..	..	..	..	..	..	..	..	..	..	..	..	..	9
Balawa	..	..	..	..	..	..	..	..	..	..	..	..	..	..	..	..	4	..	..	..	..	..	..	..	..	..	..	..	..	..	..	..	..	..	..	..	..	..	..	..	4
Bea	...	...	...	...	..	...	...	..	...	..	..	..	..	...	...	..	1	..	..	..	..	..	..	..	..	..	..	..	..	..	..	..	..	..	..	..	..	..	..	..	1
Estimated { Jarawas	..	..	..	..	..	..	..	..	..	..	..	..	..	..	..	..	..	..	..	..	..	..	..	..	30	35	22	27	31	36	23	27	..	..	..	..	..	..	..	..	231
Estimated { Önges	..	..	..	..	..	..	..	..	..	..	..	..	..	..	..	..	..	..	..	..	..	..	..	..	..	..	..	..	..	..	..	..	27	18	8	8	117	82	52	34	346
Total	25	25	9	6	17	25	8	2	1	3	..	..	17	16	2	7	14	12	1	2	10	7	..	..	30	35	22	27	31	36	23	27	27	18	8	8	117	82	52	34	786

As regards present distribution of the various tribes I give herewith a copy of the distribution map published with my Census Report of 1911. This gives the tribal areas as recognized at that time. At the present time the numbers of most of the tribes has so dwindled that it is a farce to talk about tribal areas in their connection. The Kols have disappeared, and there is to-day only one representative of the Beas, at one time the most numerous and powerful tribe in South Andaman. A perusal, however, of the table showing the location of the Andamanese enumerated, proves that they still cling feebly to their respective tribal areas. Most of the Chariars and Koras are to be found in the Temple Sound camp, (originally established on Landfall Island). The Tabo and Yere are mostly found in Stewart Sound, and on Interview Island; whereas all the remaining Bojigyabs and Balawas, and three of the five surviving Juwais, are found in the Havelock camp.

Rutland, which was at one time the home of a section of the Jarawa tribe, has now been for some years occupied by the Önges from the north of Little Andaman. The Önges first used the Island merely as a camping ground on their journeys to visit the Home in the Settlement, but they have gradually established themselves there, and even show a tendency to cross McPherson's Strait, and spread into South Andaman.

The distribution of the Jarawas remains the same as at the last Census; that is to say they occupy North Sentinel, and most of South Andaman, from the confines of the Settlement northwards as far as Middle Strait, occasionally crossing into Baratang.

	Andamanese.		
	M.	F.	Total.
1911	628	689	1,317
1921	414	372	786

(B) Movement.

The results of this year's Census of the Andamanese confirms the conclusion arrived at in 1911 that the race was dying out.

The direction and degree of movement will be considered separately in relation to:—(1) the Yerewa and Bojigngiji Groups, (2) the Önges, and (3) the Jarawas.

(a) The Yerewa and Bojigngiji Groups.

I give herewith a statement showing in figures, as well as in the form of a graph the movement in the above groups during the last twenty years. At the last Census these friendly tribes showed a decline of 27·2 % on the figures of 1901; whereas the present Census shows a further decline of 54 % in the last decade. At this rate these tribes will very shortly disappear altogether. The tribes of the Bojigngiji Group are already practically wiped out, and will probably have disappeared before the next Census is taken. There are only 19 representatives of this Group, and of these 18 are adults.

In the last Census Report I dealt at some length with the causes which have combined to bring about this rapid decline; I do not propose therefore on the present occasion to do more than summarise the conclusions then arrived at, which apply equally to-day.

Briefly stated the causes of decline are:—

1. Epidemics.
2. Civilization.
3. Syphilis.

I think that probably epidemics have been the principal direct cause of the enormous reduction in the numbers of the Andamanese since we first occupied the Islands. It is impossible at the present time to form any definite idea of the original numbers of the Andamanese. Sir Richard Temple in the Census Report of 1901 estimates the original numbers of the two Groups now being considered at about 3,500. The figures of the present Census, which may be taken as virtually exact show them as numbering 209.

As a matter of fact, the Andamans are singularly free from the more serious forms of epidemics so common in India. Plague is unknown; cholera has been confined to the Forest Coolies when first imported; small-pox, on the few occasions when it has been introduced, has been quickly localized, and stamped out; but at the same time measles and influenza do occasionally appear, and their effect on the Andamanese, once the contagion has been introduced, is disastrous.

In 1877 measles was introduced into the Settlement, and before its effect on the Andamanese was realized it had spread with great rapidity all over the Islands. It is estimated that on this occasion about half the race was killed off; not so much by the disease as by its after effect.

Under normal conditions a healthy race suffering a setback of this kind would in the course of a few years recover; Nature would automatically fill the vacuum created; but in the case of the Andamanese there were already other factors in operation which tended to make recovery impossible.

A race which does nothing towards increasing or conserving the natural food supply of the country which it occupies, and has at the same time to live on what it can get out of the country, requires a very large area per head of population to wander over if every man is to get enough to eat by hunting and fishing. In any case the population must, in the nature of things, be very sparse. Where, as in the case of the Andamanese, the area over which the race can spread is restricted, one would expect nature to provide some automatic check on overpopulation. That in the case of the Andamanese there was some such natural check is I think, proved by the fact that, so far as is known, they have never restorted to artificial means of preventing overpopulation, such as polyandry, child murder, or the procuring of abortion. In the absence of vital statistics it is impossible to say what form this check took, but the end was probably achieved through a high death rate, and a tendency towards sterility; probably the former was the principal factor.

As a result of contact with civilization the Andamanese have acquired certain bad habits. They have learnt to smoke, to drink, when they get the chance, and to take opium, when they can get it. By keeping them so far as possible away from the Settlement the opportunities for obtaining liquor and opium are restricted; but they will always smoke tobacco in excess. They have also acquired other habits which if not exactly bad in themselves have had disastrous effects on the physique of the race. By nature the Andamanese goes naked, and lives in a rude shelter of leaves which gives free access to fresh air. As a result of contact with civilization he has acquired the habit of occasionally wearing clothes, of sleeping under blankets, and of living in ill-ventilated huts; the result has been the introduction of every kind of pulmonary and bronchial complaint, which tends to encourage an even higher rate of mortality than is natural in the race.

In 1878 syphilis was introduced; the first contamination is said to have occurred through the medium of a convict, but it was some time before its presence among the Andamanese was first discovered, and by that time it had obtained such a hold on the race that its localization was no longer possible, and in spite of every effort it spread throughout the group here dealt with. The result is that the majority of marriages are now-a-days infructuous.

With a high death rate, and infertile parents it is not to be wondered at that the Andamanese of the friendly tribes are dying out.

(*b*) THE ÖNGES.

The numbers of the Önges are arrived at largely by estimate, and it is impossible to say with any degree of certainty whether they are increasing or decreasing in numbers. What evidence there is tends to show that they are decreasing. Mr. Bonig, who has probably had more communication with the Önges than any living persons, is of opinion that there are many fewer on Little Andaman to-day than there were when he first visited the Island many years ago. This opinion is borne out by the fact that the number of communal huts to be seen on the coasts of Little Andaman is considerably less than was formerly the case. Also the numbers of that section of the tribe which is located on Rutland have gone down during the last decade by 25 %. This evidence is not, I admit, very satisfactory, but it is all I have on which to base my estimate of the movement of the population.

As stated in the Chapter on the Census I have formed the opinion that the estimate of the numbers of the Önges in 1911 was too high. I have assumed a new estimate of the numbers at the last Census, and have based my estimate of the present number on an assumed reduction of 25 % on that figure.

What the reasons for this decrease, (if there really is a decrease), may be it is impossible to say with any degree of certainty. The Önges have come very much less in contact with civilization than the friendly tribes in Great Andaman. It is only that section of the tribe which is located in Rutland which ever visits the Andaman Home in Port Blair; and even their visits are as a rule of very brief duration; they have not as yet taken to wearing superfluous clothes, or to living in other than their natural huts.

It is possible of course that in their visits to the Andaman Homes they may have contracted syphilis from the other Andamanese, but in view of the apparent mutual hostility of the Septs it would not, one would think, spread very rapidly. It is conceivable of course that they have suffered from the ravages of influenza; possibly also the contagion of measles was carried to them at some time by one of the parties visiting the Settlement. However, until we are better acquainted with the Önges any estimate of the movement of the population, and the reasons therefor must be largely a matter of conjecture.

(c) The Jarawas.

About the Jarawas, and the conditions prevailing among them we know even less than in the case of the Önges.

In 1911 the numbers of this tribe were very much less than at the time of the 1901 Census. The numbers in 1901 were undoubtedly placed much too high. At the same time there is no doubt that the numbers of the Jarawas fell appreciably during that period. The section of the tribe which occupied the forests to the south of the Settlement, and the Island of Rutland, disappeared, partly no doubt through natural causes, but partly through coming in contact with the Önges, who were beginning to establish themselves on Rutland. We have, however, no evidence to show that there has been any further decrease in the numbers of the Jarawas during the last decade, and I, therefore, treat their numbers as stationary.

IV. The Nicobars.

The Nicobar Islands are situated in a rectangle formed by Long. E. 92°50′, and Long. E. 99°, and Lat. N. 9°50′, and Lat. N. 6°50′. (A) Distribution.

If we exclude the Shom Pen, a tribe in the interior of the Island of Great Nicobar, whose origin is still obscure, the Nicobarese form one race, of uniform Mongolian origin, but divided by physical characteristics, language, and habits and customs into groups; each group occupying a separate island, or group of islands. The lines of division by language does not correspond in every case with the lines of division by habits and customs; but for purposes of consideration in this Report the grouping by language has been adopted in preference to grouping by custom.

The groups are:—

1. Car Nicobar.
2. Chaura.
3. Teressa and Bompoka.
4. Nancowry, Camorta, Trinkat, Katchall. } The Central Group.
5. Great Nicobar, Little Nicobar, Pulo Milo, Kondul. } The Southern Group.
6. The Shom Pen in the interior of Great Nicobar.

The Nicobarese language has been classified by Grierson as belonging to the Mon Khmer group, and there is little doubt that the Nicobarese race is descended from Talaing emigrants from the Tenasserim coast. When these Talaings first came to the Islands it is not possible to say, but from Ptolemy's description of the islanders in his voyages it is clear that two thousand years ago the Nicobarese were in occupation of these Islands.

The theory that they are descended from emigrants from the Burmese coast coincides with the islanders' own ancient tradition. Their animistic beliefs, and their methods of propitiating the spirits which inhabit the jungles, are very similar to those encountered among the hill tribes in Burma ; and many of their ceremonies are analogous to those obtaining in Burma ; as for instance, the rites practised in Car Nicobar in connection with the burial of the revered dead, more particularly in the tug-of-war over the bier.

On the other hand the language contains a marked Malay element, which Grierson attributes to borrowed words ; and also among the customs of the Nicobarese are some which are obviously of Malay origin ; as for instance, the practice of male couvade, or the lying in of the man at the time of his wife's confinement, together with other practices in the nature of " suggestive magic " such as severing the lashings of canoe fastenings in order to make delivery easier, and to ease the birth pains.

This strong Malay element in the language and habits of the people may possibly have been derived from intercourse with the Malays, who at one time probably came to the Islands in large numbers ; but I think, this is improbable. It is a little difficult at the present time to gauge the influence on the Nicobarese of their intercourse with the Malays. The Malays disappeared from the Islands at the time of our first occupation, and the stamping out of piracy, that is to say, about 1869, and he has not returned since. At the present time all trade between the Nicobars and the Malay Peninsula and Islands is in the hands of Chinese from Penang and Singapore.

In the northern Islands the Nicobarese have very little of the Malay in their physical appearance; but as we go south the type approximates more nearly to that of the Malay, till in the Shom Pen in the interior of Great Nicobar we find a race typically Malay in appearance.

There is at the present time not very much communication between the Nicobarese in Great Nicobar and the Shom Pen. The Nicobarese live in constant dread of Shom Pen raids ; at the same time there is a certain process of fusion going on between the two races. One sometimes finds a Nicobarese with a Shom Pen wife, or Shom Pen children adopted into a Nicobarese family. This would account for the predominance of the Malay type in the south, and possibly for the Malay element in the language, though this is uncertain ; but the presence in the Great Nicobar of the Shom Pen could hardly account for the Malay strain in Car Nicobar which is separated from Great Nicobar by about 120 miles of sea. In appearance the Car Nicobarese are certainly more similar to the Burmese than to the Malays ; but on the other hand they practise male couvade, a custom they certainly did not bring with them from Burma, and their somewhat complicated method of preparing and cooking pandanus bread, the staple indigenous farinaceous food of the Islands, is exactly the same as that practised by the Shom Pen.

A possible explanation is that the Shom Pen at one time occupied all the Islands and that they were gradually driven out, by the more virile immigrants from Tenasserim, from all except Great Nicobar where the last remnant still hold out in the forests of the interior.

At the present time the Nicobarese are scattered over the islands of the Group in varying degrees of density, according to the physical characteristics of the land. In the north, where the Islands are flat, the soil comparatively rich, and the conditions suitable for the cultivation of cocoanuts, the population is comparatively dense ; whereas as one goes south the physical characteristics of the country change and the population becomes more sparse ; till in Great Nicobar, which is mountainous throughout, we find only 85 persons (exclusive of Shom Pen) in an area of 330 square miles.

Table showing density of population in inhabited Islands.

Islands.	Area in sq. miles.	Population.	Density per sq. mile.
Car Nicobar	49	6,352	130
Chaura	3	234	78
Teressa	34	596	12
Bompoka	4	83	21
Camorta	58	575	10
Nancowry	19	172	9
Trinkat	6	68	11
Katchall	62	341	5·5
Great Nicobar	333	460	1·3
Little Nicobar	58	33	·6
Kondul	½	72	144
Pulo Milo	½	31	62

(B) Movement.

Year.	Nicobarese.	Shom Pen (estimated).	Officials and Traders.	Crews of Ships.	Total Population.
1901	5,962	348	201	...	6,511
1911	7,991	375	351	95	8,812
1921	8,248	375	394	243	9,260

The Census of 1921 shows an increase in the population of the Nicobars of 448 persons. For this increase the Traders are responsible for 191, and the indigenous population has increased by 257.

There is no doubt that on the whole the population of the Nicobars is increasing ; but the movement is not evenly distributed ; it varies in the different groups, some of which are actually on the decrease ; but the increase in one direction more than compensates for the decrease in others.

In considering the movement of the population the figures will be dealt with by groups rather than as a whole because the conditions affecting the question are different in the various groups.

Statement showing movement of the population in the Nicobars by Groups, from 1901—1921.

Islands.	Year.	No. of. Houses.	Nicobarese.			Officials and Traders.			Grand Total.
			M.	F.	Total.	M.	F.	Total.	
Car Nicobar	1901	748	1,830	1,621	3,451	201	...	201	3,652
	1911	768	2,892	2,658	5,550	237	7	244	5,794
	1921	1,098	3,268	2,819	6,087	250	15	265	6,352
Chaura	1901	130	272	250	522	...	...	...	522
	1911	92	196	152	348	...	...	...	348
	1921	82	141	93	234	...	...	...	234
Teressa and Bompoka	1901	130	382	320	702	...	...	...	702
	1911	139	357	299	656	36	...	36	692
	1921	147	332	308	640	39	...	39	679
Central Group	1901	235	561	534	1,095	...	...	...	1,095
	1911	225	613	552	1,165	63	3	66	1,231
	1921	220	591	480	1,071	85	...	85	1,156
Southern Group	1901	54	99	93	192	...	...	...	192
	1911	37	151	121	272	5	...	5	277
	1921	29	94	122	216	5	...	5	221
Shom Pen (Estimated)	1901	...	192	156	348	...	...	...	348
	1911	...	190	185	375	...	...	...	375
	1921	...	190	185	375	...	...	...	375
Crews of Vessels enumerated in Nicobars.	1911	6	...	...	...	95	...	95	95
	1921	11	...	...	...	243	...	243	243

(a) Car Nicobar.

Of the total population of the Nicobars more than two-thirds is concentrated in Car Nicobar.

The Island is comparatively flat, the soil is rich, and eminently suited to the cultivation of cocoanuts (the currency of the Nicobars); the climate is reasonably healthy: and the conditions generally are more favourable for the support of a dense population than is the case in any of the other Islands. The result is apparent in the large and increasing population found on Car Nicobar.

Year.	No. of huts.	Nicobarese.			Traders.			Total.
		M.	F.	Total.	M.	F.	Total.	
1911 . . .	768	2,892	2,658	5,550	237	7	244	5,794
1921 . . .	1,098	3,268	2,819	6,087	250	15	265	6,352

That the population is increasing is now quite clear, and the average rate of progress is also fairly clear.

A rough Census of the Island was taken in 1883, and the indigenous population was estimated at 3,500. The Census of 1901 however showed a slight falling-off in the number of Nicobarese on the Island. The Census of 1911 on the other hand showed an increase of over 2,000, that is to say a rise of over 60 per cent. in ten years, which was obviously impossible. In my report of 1911 I opined that the figures for 1901 were not true, in support of which view I gave certain reasons. I further assumed that the figures for 1883 were approximately correct, and that there had been a steady increase from that time onwards; I estimated that the true figures for 1901 must have been somewhere about 4,830. The results of the present Census confirms this view.

The actual population of Car Nicobar was found to be 6,352 persons, but there are good grounds for believing that the figure would have been higher had not the Island been visited by an epidemic of influenza of the most virulent type during June and July of 1920, which resulted in the death of a large number of persons. The Government Agent, who was himself attacked, was unable to keep any return of the number of deaths, but as the result of subsequent enquiries he estimated that about 490 had died. Had influenza not visited the Island it is probable that the population at the time of the Census would have been about 6,800.

There is no doubt therefore that the population is increasing rapidly, and that the question of overpopulation is a problem which will have to be faced some day. The Island is in my opinion however capable of supporting a very much larger population than is found there to-day. Cocoanuts in the Nicobars take the place of gold in more civilized communities; it is the source of wealth, and the currency of the country. Car Nicobar produces vast quantities of cocoanuts, of which a very large number are wasted by the inhabitants. A very large proportion of those expended in trade are used to buy what are really luxuries, and they are not moreover sold at present for their full market value. It is probable that much of the land not now under cultivation can be made to grow cocoanuts. There is in other words a considerable surplus of wealth on the Island which can be drawn upon.

With reasonable economy the existing resources of the Island are I think sufficient to provide for a much larger population than are at present dependent on them.

(b) Chaura.

Table showing movement of population in Chaura.

Year.	No. of huts.	Nicobarese.			Traders.			Total.
		M.	F.	Total.	M.	F.	Total.	
1911 . . .	92	196	152	348	...	...	...	348
1921 . . .	82	141	93	234	...	...	...	234

The population of Chaura has decreased during the last decade by 114 persons, a reduction of 33 per cent.

In 1883 De Roepstorff enumerated no less than 690 persons on the Island. The Census party of 1901 found 522 ; in 1911 I enumerated 348 ; to-day there are only 234 ; that is to say, only about one-third of the number in 1883.

It is obvious from these figures that the population of Chaura is declining very rapidly. At the time of the last Census it was thought that the apparently rapid decline was in part attributable to an epidemic, the exact nature of which was not known, which has visited the Island the previous year; but this year's figures go to prove that the decline is steady and continuous.

The Island of Chaura occupies a peculiar position in the body politic of the Nicobars. It is a small Island with a comparatively dense population, and produces only enough cocoanuts for its own consumption ; in consequence there is no trade, and circumstances have made it necessary for the people of Chaura to obtain in some other way the trade articles which the inhabitants of other islands procure in exchange for cocoanuts.

By some means which cannot now be traced the people of Chaura have gained a moral ascendancy over the inhabitants of the other islands, who look upon Chaura as the abode of evil spirits, and believe that the people of the Island have a peculiar power of influencing the said devils.

Possibly, necessity being the mother of invention, the Chaura men were the first to discover the art of pottery, and to make capital out of the invention. Be that as it may, the manufacture of clay cooking pots is " tabu " on every island except Chaura, whereas the spirits have decreed that pig and certain other forms of food may be cooked *only* in these earthenware Chaura pots, and the Nicobarese, from Car Nicobar in the north to Great Nicobar in the south, are forced to make long voyages to Chaura in their frail canoes to purchase their annual supply of these pots, for which they pay with the trade articles which Chaura would otherwise have to do without.

For how long this law has been in operation it is impossible now to say, its origin is lost in the mists of time ; but that it is no recent enactment is proved by the fact that the supply of clay on the Island was exhausted long years ago, and the men of Chaura must voyage in their canoes to the neighbouring Island of Teressa to procure the clay to make the pots to sell, among others, to the people of Teressa.

In addition to the pot trade the Island of Chaura has acquired the monopoly of the sale of the large racing canoes to Car Nicobar. That Island being rich requires a large number of these canoes, which, there being on the Island no timber suitable for their manufacture, have to be obtained from the Central or Southern Groups, where they are made. The people of Chaura insist on the deal being carried out through them, and pocket a handsome middle-man's commission on the transaction.

It is impossible to say definitely how the people of Chaura won for themselves the peculiar position they now hold in the Islands. Possibly Chaura was the first Island to be occupied, and as her children emigrated to establish new communities on other islands she continued to exercise over them the rights of a parent to dictate to her offspring.

The peculiar position of Chaura in the economic system does not help us to explain the rapid downward movement in the population.

There is no doubt that Chaura was at one time comparatively densely populated. De Roepstorff's figures for 1883 make the density at that time 230 to the square mile, and there is no reason to suppose that the decline in the population only commenced after that date ; so that it is fairly safe to assume that the Island was at one time faced with the problem of over-population, and it is highly probable that the people resorted to artificial means to prevent this ; in fact we have fairly clear proof that this is so. We have incontestable proof that the procuring of abortion is practised by the women of the Central Group ; not so much to prevent over-population, as because they wish to avoid the pains and responsibilities of childbirth ; and in every case that has come under my notice Chaura women, living in the Central Islands were implicated. It is hardly likely that the women of Chaura would have the reputation of being especially skilful in the matter of procuring abortion unless it were practised on the Island. We know so little of what goes on in Chaura that it is impossible to say to what extent the procuring of abortion is practised to-day; but it may be safely surmised that it is one of the principal, if not the principal cause of the decline in the population.

In the case of a community living in the conditions which obtain to-day in Chaura one would expect to find emigration going on. Looking through the Census returns I found 122 persons born on Chaura domiciled on Islands of the Central Group. There is no doubt that the tendency to emigrate is greater in the case of the people of Chaura than in the case of inhabitants of other Islands; but the small number found on other Islands, which must represent emigration over a number of years, is not sufficient to explain more than a very small proportion of the decline in the population of Chaura.

It is a peculiar fact, for which I can offer no explanation, that the emigrants from Chaura are all found on the Islands of the Central Group, and not one on Teressa; whereas Teressa is distant from Chaura only a few miles, and the inhabitants are more nearly allied to those of Chaura by language habits, and customs than to the people of any other Island or Group, and one would naturally have expected the surplus population of Chaura to have found its way there in the first instance.

Except for the prevalence of elephantiasis, which may possibly be attributable to past overcrowding, the inhabitants of Chaura appear reasonably healthy; but the number of old men and women appears to be low, and it is quite possible that the death rate is high.

There are no doubt many causes contributory to the decline in the population of Chaura; but I believe the principal one to be the procuring of abortion.

(c) Teressa and Bompoka.

Statement showing movement of population in Teressa and Bompoka.

Year.	No. of huts.	Nicobarese.			Traders.			Total.
		M.	F.	Total.	M.	F.	Total.	
1911 . . .	139	357	299	656	36	...	36	692
1921 . . .	147	332	308	640	39	...	39	679

The population of Teressa and Bompoka is practically stationary.

There is no reason apparent why the population should not increase; generally speaking, conditions on the Island are favourable to an increasing population. The reason for the lack of movement is possibly the climate, which is none too healthy. Possibly also the procuring of abortion is practised; a state of things which I suspected at the time of the last Census, but of which I have still no proof.

(d) The Central Group.

Statement showing movement of population in the Central Group.

Year.	No. of huts.	Nicobarese.			Traders.			Total.
		M.	F.	Total.	M.	F.	Total.	
1911 . . .	225	613	552	1,165	63	3	66	1,231
1921 . . .	220	591	480	1,071	85	...	85	1,156

The population of the Central Group is I think practically stationary. There is a small drop in the numbers enumerated, but not sufficiently pronounced to indicate a decline in the population; more particularly as the numbers are slightly higher this year than they were in 1901.

The reason for this stationary population is probably the same as indicated in the case of Teressa. The climate is extremely malarious, and a high death rate is to be expected. We know also that the procuring of abortion is practised among the women. The presence at Nancowry of the Assistant Government Agent enables us to get a clearer idea of what is going on in the Central Group than is possible in the case of any of the other Islands except Car Nicobar. At the time of the last Census the wife of the late Agent, Rati Lal, who was father of the present Agent, was still alive. She had considerable experience of the Islands, was a women of strong character, and had great influence with the Nicobarese, which she used to combat this practice of procuring abortion, and I was able to obtain from her much interesting information on the subject. Whether her efforts have had any effect, or whether even the practice was ever sufficiently universal to affect the movement of the population it is difficult to say. The number of cases reported would not indicate its being so; but it is possible that only a small percentage of the cases which occur are reported.

(e) The Southern Group.

Table showing movement of population in Southern Group.

Year.	No. of huts.	Nicobarese.			Traders.			Total.
		M.	F.	Total.	M.	F.	Total.	
1911 . . .	37	151	121	272	5	...	5	277
1921 . . .	29	94	122	216	5	...	5	221

The figures of the last Census of this Group showed an increase on those of the previous Census; but I opined that the numbers for 1901, which were not obtained by direct enumeration, were too low, and I estimated that the population of these Islands was in reality decreasing. The results of this Census go to show that my estimate of the movement was correct.

To one who like myself has known these Islands for a number of years it is obvious, without reference to the Census figures, that the population is decreasing; numbers of villages have disappeared, and no new ones have opened in their place. The disappearance of the villages is not of course due to the complete wiping out of the inhabitants; it is due to the gradual process of dwindling, until the numbers become so small that the survivors move to some larger village where they enjoy greater immunity from the expected raids of the dreaded Shom Pen. This process has been going on for years, till the whole population of Great Nicobar that has not moved to one or other of the small islands, where they are immune from attack, is concentrated at the little harbour of Pulo Babi on the west coast of the Island.

At the time of the last Census I came to the conclusion that the Shom Pen menace was more imaginary than real, and the experience of the last ten years has tended to confirm me in this view. At the same time the Nicobarese still live in constant dread of attack and I believe this to be one of the factors influencing the movement question. The Southern Islands, and Great Nicobar in particular, are unquestionably unpopular. Not only is there the Shom Pen menace to be reckoned with, rendering as it does the accumulation of property inadvisable, as offering a temptation to the raiders; but owing to the presence on the Island of large flocks of monkeys it is not possible to cultivate vegetable gardens, or to grow fruit as in the case of the other Groups; the result is that sons and daughters both marry away, and there is little young stock to replace the old people when they die. However, when all is said and done, it is probably the climate which more than anything else accelerates the downward tendency in the population. The climate of Great and Little Nicobars is even more malarious than that of the Central Group, and it may be taken for granted that the death rate is proportionately higher.

(f) The Shom Pen.

I have been able to learn nothing of this tribe beyond what was known at the last Census, and the population is treated as stationary.

APPENDIX A.

General and special orders issued by the Superintendent, Census Operations, in connection with the Census of 1921.

CENSUS 1921.

GENERAL ORDERS.

The Census will be taken on the evening of the 18th March, 1921.

The arrangements will generally speaking be the same as in 1911.

For the purposes of the census, the administration will be divided into the three Districts, *viz.* :—

I. The Settlement of Port Blair.

II. The Andamans outside the Settlement.

III. The Nicobars.

The Census of the Settlement will be synchronous and will be carried out in accordance with the procedure laid down in the Imperial Census Code. A District Census Officer being appointed to make the necessary arrangements.

The Census of the Andamans outside the Settlement will be divided into two parts :—

(1) The Census of the aboriginal tribes.

(2) The Census of the Forest Camps.

The Census of the aborigines will be non-synchronous, and will be arranged for by the Officer-in-charge of Andamanese.

The Census of Forest Camps will be synchronous, and will be carried out with the assistance of the Forest Department in accordance with the procedure laid down in the Imperial Census Code.

The Census of the Nicobars.

The Census of the Nicobars will be non-synchronous.

The Census of Car Nicobar will be taken by the Government Agent on that Island during the month of February.

The Census of Teressa and Bompoka and of the Central Group will be taken at the same time by the Assistant Agent, Nancowry.

The Census of Chaura and of the Southern Group will be taken by the Census Superintendent himself in the course of a trip to the Islands between the 3rd and the 15th March.

R. F. LOWIS,

28th December, 1920. *Deputy Commissioner, Port Blair.*

THE CENSUS OF THE SETTLEMENT.

(1) For the purposes of the Census of the Settlement, the Revenue Assistant Commissioner will be appointed as District Census Officer.

(2) The Settlement will be divided into 5 charges, the boundaries of which will coincide with the recognised District boundaries.

(3) Each District Officer will act as charge Superintendent in his own District.

(4) The Troops of the Garrison, including all followers who are not convicts, and the Military Police Battallion will be dealt with separately, the Census in each unit being arranged for by the Commanding Officer in accordance with rules for the taking of the Census in Cantonments.

(5) For the purposes of taking the Census each charge, that is to say each Administrative District, will be treated as a Circle and sub-divided into blocks. Blocks will be of two kinds :—

(I) Village blocks, (II) Station blocks.

(6) The villages of the Settlement are small, well defined, and self-contained, and each village will form one block. The bazars of Ross and Aberdeen will be treated as separate blocks.

(7) Each convict station and the residential houses in its vicinity will be treated as one block Station blocks will be as follows :—

JAIL DISTRICT.

Block I.—The Cellular and Associated Jails, including free Supervising staff and families.

Block II.—The Female Jail, including Supervising staff and families.

Ross District.

Block I.—Ross convict station and all residential bungalows on the Island.

Block II.—Middle Point station and all residential bungalows between Cellular Jail and Aberdeen Bazar, and all houses to the East and South of the Main Road from Aberdeen Jetty to Phœnix Bay including the Wireless station.

Block III.—Aberdeen station.

Haddo District.

Block I.—Phœnix Bay station and all bungalows on the Phœnix Bay ridge, and the Marine Department quarters including free crews of Marine Department launches.

Block II.—Haddo station and all residential quarters on the Haddo Peninsular.

Block III.—Chatham, including all Forest Department employees and free crews of Forest Department steamers and launches.

Block IV.—Navy Bay station with all residential bungalows in that area.

Block V.—Pahargaon.

Wimberley Gunj District.

Block I.—Bamboo Flat station including Medical staff attached to Bamboo Flat Hospital.

Block II.—Wimberley Gunj station including Stewart Gunj Farm and Forest Department employees.

Block III.—Gobang station including rubber plantation.

Viper District.

Block I.—Viper station with all residential houses on the Island.

Block II.—Dundas Point station.

Block III.—Namunaghar station.

Block IV.—Port Mouat station.

(8) For the enumeration of village blocks enumerators will be appointed by the District Census Officer (Revenue Assistant Commissioner) in consultation with the District Officers.

(9) In station blocks the Jailor or Tahsildar Overseer in charge of the station will be *ex-officio* enumerator. The actual enumeration of all convicts will be carried out by station Munshis and the returns checked in the District offices. The Jailor and Tahsildar Overseers will themselves only be responsible for the distribution and filling up household schedules at the various houses in their blocks.

(10) In the household schedules issued to householaers will be enumerated, besides the occupant and his family, all free servants actually resident in the bungalow. A free servants domiciled in a village, will be enumerated in the village in which he resides. Convict servants whether resident in the house or not will be enumerated at the station to which they belong.

(11) The preliminary enumeration should commence about 1st February, and should be complete by the 1st March, so far as possible transfers of convicts between Districts should be restricted between the 1st February and the 18th March and should be stopped between the 10th and 18th March.

(12) On completion of the Preliminary Census the District Census Officer will prepare and submit to the Census Superintendent a District Circle Register in the following form :—

Circle Register.

Name of Village or Station.	Serial No. of Block.	No. of occupied Houses in Block.		Name of Enumerator.	Date of Preliminary Record.	
		Houses.	Barracks.		Commencement.	Completion.

(13) The final enumeration, that is to say the checking and bringing up to date of the record prepared at the preliminary enumeration, will commence at 7 P.M. on the 18th March, and should be completed by midnight.

(14) On the morning after the Census enumerators will proceed with their books to the Deputy Commissioner's Office at 8 A.M. The District Census Officer will compare the number of books received with the number of blocks shown in the Circle Register. He will satisfy himself that all household schedules have been collected. He will then have the number of houses, males and females in each block added up independently by the enumerator of the block, and by two other enumerators; when the totals thus arrived at agree, they may be accepted as correct and a Circle Summary prepared in the following form :—

CIRCLE SUMMARY.

Name of Village or Station.	Serial No. of Block.	No. of occupied houses.	Persons.		
			Total.	Male.	Female.

The totals of the 5 Circle Summaries added together will be handed to the Census Superintendent for inclusion in the total for the whole administration.

January, 1921.

R. F. LOWIS,
Census Superintendent.

APPENDIX B.

Report of District Census Officer, together with orders issued by him in connection with the Census of the Settlement.

No. 5-C. F., dated Port Blair, the 7th April, 1921.

From—BUNYAD HUSSAIN, Esq., B.A., Punjab Civil Service, District Census Officer, Port Blair,
To—R. F. LOWIS, Esq., Census Superintendent, Port Blair.

I have the honour to submit my report on the Census Operations in the Settlement of Port Blair.

2. The division of the Settlement into blocks had already been provided from the orders issued by you. It remained only for me to arrange for house numbering and appoint enumerators for the various blocks.

3. I submit herewith a copy of the supplementary instructions issued by me and give below a brief summary.

The house numbering began on 25th December, 1920 and finished on 31st December, 1920.

The preliminary enumeration commenced on the 10th February and completed on the 28th February, 1921.

The following plan was adopted. I convened a meeting at my place (Haddo) of the Tahsildar Overseers, Head Clerks, the Patwaris and the station Munshis of all the five districts. Instructed them how to fill up forms, especially the columns 4, 8 and 12.

Each convict station Munshi was appointed to enumerate his station and each Head Clerk was held responsible for the accuracy of the returns of his District.

The Patwaris were ordered to enumerate the villages of their respective circles under the supervision of the Tahsildar Overseer. Patwari of the Pahargaon circle to enumerate Ross and Aberdeen Bazars in addition.

Household schedules were distributed among the Gazetted Officers.

The Jailors were directed to secure the returns from the non-Gazetted Officials, free Christian families and convict Christians.

The majority of the convict station Munshis could not be relied on to fill in correctly the schedules. I adopted the following arrangements.

I ordered them to prepare for the convicts in their respective stations manuscript schedules in the same form as the standard schedule forms and to fill up columns 1, 3, 5, 6, 12, 13, 14, 15 and 16.

They were further asked to forward the manuscript schedules when complete to the District Head Clerks, who were directed to fill up the remaining columns by consulting the History sheets, Nominal Rolls, etc., in the District Office and to send them on to me duly completed by the 1st March, 1921.

The Patwaris were directed to make entries into the schedules in the first instance.

I received the manuscript schedules on the 1st March. As anticipated there were numerous mistakes and erasures.

On the 2nd March I called all the five Patwaris at my place, Haddo. Deputed eight more convict writers to assist them. All of them worked here between 2nd March and 22nd March, 1921 under my supervision and that of the Tahsildar Overseer Faqir Jalaluddin; first on checking the manuscript schedules and later on copying the entries into standard schedule forms. This was done satisfactorily.

Transfers of convicts between Districts were restricted to the minimum between 1st and 18th March. But as a matter of fact I ignored all such transfers and to bring the returns up to date—I asked the District Officers to furnish me with a statement regarding the runaways, recaptures, deceased and released convicts.

4. On the 18th the final enumeration day the following arrangements were adopted:—

The manuscript schedules were returned to the station Munshis with the instruction that they should bring them up to date.

As the alterations were expected to be very few they were asked to make a note of changes on a separate piece of paper.

The Head Clerks were ordered to return the schedules to me with the slips containing the alterations on the morning of the 19th March.

I got back the schedules as well as the slips and the statements of runaways, recaptures, etc., referred to above on the morning of the 19th March. This enabled me to make the necessary adjustments.

The final checking of the village returns was done by the Patwaris while those of Ross and Aberdeen Bazars were checked by Munshi Naiyar Hussain, Head Munshi of the Chief Commissioner's Office, and M. Abdul Rauf, Accountant, Haddo Office, respectively.

The totalling and examination of schedules occupied up till the 22nd March, 1921.

5. I shall submit separately the names of the persons who rendered valuable assistance in this connection.

Copy of Order, dated 24th December, 1920, from the Revenue Assistant Commissioer, to the Patwaris of the Four Districts.

Regarding Census, 1921.

The Deputy Commissioner has directed me to inform you to do numbering work with ordinary charcoal.

Take your chainman and number the houses with ordinary charcoal before the 31st instant and submit the report.

The Deputy Commissioner will inspect this work some day in January, if possible.

(Sd.) BUNYAD HUSSAIN,
Revenue Assistant Commissioner, Port Blair.

Copy of No. 81-C.F., from the District Census Officer, to all District Officers, dated 9th February, 1921.

A copy of the printed instructions issued by the Census Superintendent is enclosed herewith for your information.

II.—The preliminary enumeration to begin at once. Village blocks and Residential houses will be enumerated by the Patwaris. The convict stations will be done by the station Munshis under the direct supervision of the Head clerk of each District.

The Patwaris have been instructed how to fill up forms, etc. It will save much trouble if the Head Clerk collects all Munshis and calls the Patwari to train them. The Patwaris have been directed to render all assistance possible.

The Head Clerk must be impressed that he will be held responsible for the mathematical accuracy of the returns.

III.—I am sending herewith a copy of the sample of Enumerator's book to be transmitted to the Head Clerk with the following instructions :—

He must—

(1) carefully study the instructions given on the covering for filling up the schedules and those contained in this note ;

(2) ask the Patwari of his District for the convict station Block list ;

(NOTE—.M. Azizud-din for Cellular Jail, Ross and Haddo Districts, Babu Gajadhar for Viper District and Babu Jawala Singh for Wimberley Gunj District.)

(3) get necessary stationery from District Office and distribute it among the station Munshis ;

(4) open a register for each convict station attaching at the top all the headings given in the General Schedule ;

(5) direct the station Munshis to fill up column Nos. 1, 3, 5, 6, 12, 13, 14, 15 and 16 on the spot very carefully visiting each barrack ;

(6) direct the station Munshis to complete the information required in paragraph (5) above by the 19th instant and return the registers duly filled in to him ;

(7) fill up the remaining columns *excepting No. 2* after consulting the History sheets, Nominal rolls, etc., in the office and complete this information by the 28th instant ;

(8) see that the total number of convicts (deducting the self-supporters in the villages) given in the registers tallies with the total number shown on the books of his District ;

(9) send the registers duly completed to me on or before the 1st March, 1921.

IV.—I beg to invite your attention to paragraph (II) of the printed instructions mentioned in paragraph 1 above. I shall be much obliged if the transfers of the convicts be restricted to the minimum between now and the 10th March and stopped absolutely afterwards up to the 18th March, 1921. Many erasures and corrections will thereby be saved.

V.—As mentioned above the Patwaris will be able to remove doubts. If they cannot, they have been directed to refer to me. It will much facilitate work if the Head Clerk and the Patwari work in consultation.

VI.—The following instructions will be found useful :—

(1) The station Munshis not to start work until they get block list from the Patwari.

(2) The station Munshis must know that they have to visit each barrack for obtaining the information. They must take the Jemadar with them and see that all convicts assigned to that barrack are present and that the same convicts are not transferred to another barrack prior to their visit. It can more conveniently be done after the lock-up.

(3) Each station Munshi should see that that total number of convicts of one station entered in his register tallies with the total number shown on the books of his District.

(4) In column No. 3 the name and number of the convict must be written.

(5) In column No. 9 write only the word "convict" column No. 10 should be left blank.

(6) In column No. 12 write only the name of the *district* where the convict was born: Do not write the name of Tahsil, Thana, or village.

(7) Some free persons have obtained passes for collecting bamboo materials from Ross and Haddo Districts and are working in Viper and Wimberley Gunj Districts, They will be entered by the Patwari of the village of their permanent residence.

(8) If a convict is doubtful whether his wife is alive or dead he should be entered as "Married."

(9) Station Munshis will include men belonging to their station who are either in Hospital or are temporarily transferred to other station or District.

(10) Branch convict stations will merge into the principal.

VII.—I shall be visiting each District frequently to see how the work is done.

I shall be obliged if you issue a General order to the Jailor, Overseers, Head Clerk, Munshis and Jemadars to meet me on receiving intimation from me direct and to render the necessary assistance.

(Sd.) BUNYAD HUSSAIN,
District Census Officer, Port Blair.

Copy of No. nil, dated the 12th February, 1921, from the District Census Officer, Port Blair, to the District Officers.

In continuation of this office No. 81-F., dated the 8th February, 1921, I have the honour to add as under :—

(1) Some convicts of your District are temporarily working or undergoing treatment in another district. It is obviously difficult for the station Munshi to visit each district to secure the information for a few convicts.

The best solution seems to be to write to the head of departments to furnish particulars in regard to those convicts. A statement with names and number be sent to them and they be asked to kindly fill in the other columns.

(Sd.) BUNYAD HUSSAIN,
District Census Officer, Port Blair.

Copy of No. 83-C. F., dated the 14th February, 1921, from the District Census Officer, to all District Officers.

In continuation of this office No. 81 C. F., dated the 9th February, 1921, I have the honour to supplement as under :—.

(1) In Urdu Schedules the Figures (*e.g., vide* column No. 7) shall be written in Urdu.

(2) In column No. 7 the words (Biha) if married and (Bin Biha) if unmarried will be written. The words Kunwar or Kunwari will not be written.

(3) The station Munshis need not wait for the Block list to be supplied from the Patwari. They should start work at once. They should be directed to write the Public Works Department barrack number only and should finish one barrack *in toto* before beginning another.

(Sd.) BUNYAD HUSSAIN,
District Census Officer, Port Blair.

Copy of No. 84-C. F., dated the 14th February, 1921, from the District Census Officer, to the District Officers.

I have got only a limited number of Household schedules with me. I propose, that they should be distributed only among the Gazetted Officers.

2. Will you kindly make out a list containing the names of all the Gazetted Officers of your District and despatch it at your early convenience?

3. On getting the list I will send the required number to you with the request that the schedules be passed on to each officer with your letter asking him to please fill them up on the evening of the 18th March, 1921, and return them to the Jailor or his man on the morning of the 19th March, 1921.

4. Kindly furnish a copy of the Officers' list to your Jailor also and direct him to arrange to collect the schedules from each officer on the morning of the 19th March, 1921, and to send them without delay the same morning to me *per* special messenger.

(Sd.) BUNYAD HUSSAIN,
District Census Officer, Port Blair

Copy of No. nil, dated the 15th February, 1921, from the District Census Officer, to all District Officers.

Kindly see General Schedule column Nos. 4, 7 and 8.

I understand it is not possible to get information to fill in the above columns from the History sheets particularly of old standing convicts such as 22000 and below.

Under the circumstances kindly direct the station Munshis to fill in the columns Nos. 4. 7 and 8 also on the spot.

(Sd.) BUNYAD HUSSAIN,
District Census Officer, Port Blair.

Copy of No. 86-C. F., dated the 15th February, 1921, from the District Census Officer, to all District Officers.

I propose to hold a meeting at my place at Haddo on Sunday the 20th instant at 10 A.M. to give instructions and to solve the points that may have arisen in each District.

2. I shall be obliged if you kindly order your Tahsildar-Overseer, Head Clerk, the Head Munshi, the station Munshis, to attend the meeting. They should make a note of all points they want to ask me and bring registers for my inspection.

(Sd.) BUNYAD HUSSAIN,
District Census Officer, Port Blair.

Copy of No. 90-C. F., dated the 21st February, 1921, from the District Census Officer, to all District Officers.

In continuation of this Office No. 81-C. F., dated the 9th February, 1921, I have the honour to supplement as under :—

(1) Please direct the Head Clerk to return the registers duly completed sc as to reach me by the 2nd March, 1921.

The Head Clerks are responsible for the accuracy of the information entered in all the columns especially of Nos. 8, 4 and 12. Much trouble was experienced at the last Census owing to the inaccurate information contained in the above mentioned columns.

2. Experience has shown that the return of sect for Indian Christians and Anglo-Indians will be very incomplete unless special precautions are taken befcre-hand.

I shall be obliged if you kindly make out a list of only the heads of each family of your District (officials, non-officials excluding Gazetted Officers) and let me know the number early. I shall send you the blank General Schedules with a copy of instructions to be transmitted to your Jailor. The Jailor must be directed to study carefully the instructions and be held responsible for the Schedules being correctly filled in and to return them to me duly completed by the 10th March, 1921.

(Sd.) BUNYAD HUSSAIN,
District Census Officer, Port Blair.

Copy of No. 105-C. F., dated the 8th March, 1921, from the District Census Officer, to all District Officers.

I shall be obliged if you kindly direct your Head Clerk to send a statement in the following form *without fail* straight to me *per* special messenger on the morning of the 19th instant by 10 A.M. at the latest.

The information is required only between the dates 1st and 18th March, 1921.

No. and name of run-away convicts.	No. and name of recaptured convicts.	No. and name of deceased convicts.	No. and name of released convicts.

(Sd.) BUNYAD HUSSAIN,
District Census Officer, Port Blair.

Copy of No. 106, dated the 14th March, 1921, from the District Census Officer, Port Blair, to all District Officers.

I shall return each convict station register to the Head Clerk on or before the morning of the 18th instant.

Kindly direct the Head Clerk as under :—

(1) To distribute the Registers among the station Munshis.

(2) To direct the station Munshis to check each entry by visiting each barrack on the evening of the 18th instant.

(3) To instruct the station Munshis to make a note of all changes that may have occurred in the meantime on a separate piece of paper.

(4) To collect back all the registers very early on the morning of the 19th instant. To check all the changes that were made by station Munshis.

(5) To see that the total number of convicts (deducting the self-supporters in the villages) given in the registers agrees with the total shown on the books of his District.

(6) To return all the Registers with the slips on which changes have been noted by the station Munshis to me at Haddo so as to reach *without fail* by 10 A.M. on the 19th instant. He will also send only Head Munshi of his District with the Registers who will help me in the totalling.

It should be noted that the non-receipt of even one register will delay the final totals that must be telegraphed to the Commissioner of the Census on the 19th instant.

(Sd.) BUNYAD HUSSAIN,
District Census Officer, Port Blair.

Copy of Order dated the 14th March, 1921.

To

ALL CENSUS WORKERS.

The final enumeration will be done on the 18th instant as detailed under :—

Name of block.	Name of enumerator.
(1) All villages	Patwari of their respective ilaqa. They can ask the Chaudhris and Chaukidars to render them the necessary assistance.
(2) Each convict station	Each convict station Munshis.
(3) Ross Bazar	Munshi Naiyar Hussain of the Chief Commissioner's Office assisted by convict Gazanfar Ali.
(4) Aberdeen Bazar	M. Abdul Rauf, Accountant, Haddo District Office, assisted by convict Kunj Behari.

(Sd.) BUNYAD HUSSAIN,
District Census Officer, Port Blair.

APPENDIX C.

Diaries of Superintendent, Census Operations, whilst on tour in the Andaman Islands.

FIRST CENSUS TOUR.

17th February, 1921.—Went on board S. S. "Nancowry" about 7 A.M. and after the usual delay due to late arrival of fresh stores, ice, milk, butter, etc., we finally sailed at about 8-10 A.M.

The S. L. "Sohrab" started about the same time for Havelock, but our courses diverged, and she was soon little more than a smudge of smoke on the horizon.

The wind freshened as the day advanced, and it was beginning to get a bit rough by noon when we ran into Middle Straits and calm water. I kept a look out for indications of Jarawas and about half-way through the Strait we sighted one of their old rafts. It was obviously a last year's one, from which it may be presumed that the Jarawas have not yet crossed into Baratang, as they generally do at about this time of year.

We anchored off Lekara-lunta at about 3 P.M. My information was that there were no Andamanese in this part of the Islands ; but I landed at the point where the Andamanese usually camp. There was an old camp there all right, ; but it had not been occupied for a very long time.

I shot a few pigeons for the larder, and we had a bath and returned to the Nancowry at dusk.

18th February.—After a very chilly night we started at 6-30 A.M. and leaving Port Anson, started north up the west coast of the Islands.

There had evidently been some wind in the night which we had not felt inside the harbour, for it was distinctly rough.

We made up to Interview Island at about 1 o'clock, and anchored off the Tota-ino camp. The Pahrewala in charge came off to report, bringing with him about 20 to 30 lbs of tortoise-shell collected by the Andamanese. He reported that most of the men were absent from the camp hunting and fishing, and would not be back before dark. I ascertained further from the Andamanese that there were some independent parties out in the Stewart Sound Basin; but where exactly, these were located they could not say. I was anxious to get on as quickly as possible so directed the Pahrewala to enumerate and write down the numbers of the Andamanese in his camp as soon as they came in, and to send the result by hand of one of the older and more intelligent of the men to meet me at Stewart Sound on the 22nd February; his messenger was to try and get into touch, *en route*, with the independent camps in the Stewart Sound Basin, and bring them in with him for enumeration.

Having made my arrangements we sailed again at 2 P.M. for North Reef Island.

En route we crossed a shoal patch, not marked on the chart. This is probably the same shoal on which R. I. M. S. "Elphinstone" struck in 1900. It is an extensive shoal with 3 to 4 fathoms on it, and at one point not more than 1½ fathoms. We got soundings between three and four fathoms for quite a mile; the bottom was clearly visible. North Reef itself is steep too on this side, and one has to go close in short to anchor.

We anchored at the north end of the island. Although rather late we landed. There is a fresh water lagoon on the island which sometimes has teal on it. We found the lagoon nearly dry; but there was a little water at one point, and we got three teal, and a hackle pigeon. We also had a bathe.

There were no indications of Andamanese on the island.

19th February.—Sailed at daylight. There was less sea, and we made good progress, and were in Temple Sound by 10 A.M. Here we saw some Andamanese and canoes, and discovered a large camp on Paget Island. This was the camp I had expected to find at Land Fall. The Pahrewala came off and reported that there were about 50 in the camp, but that some were out on the main-land in independent camps, hunting; he promised however to get them all in by 8 P.M., so I decided to remain in Temple Sound for the night.

At 4 P.M. we landed and I shot a few pigeon, returning to the camp at dusk, where I enumerated all present. The hunting parties had not come in, but the Pahrewala promised to bring them off to the Nancowry as soon as they arrived.

It was nearly full moon, and suitable for turtle spearing, so I arranged with the Andamanese to take us out as soon as it was quite dark, and in the meantime we watched the evening dance in extremely picturesque, if somewhat unsavoury surroundings. It was a pleasant change to find oneself half a hour later gliding in absolute silence over the smooth water of the Sound in the clean cold moonlight.

Fate was not kind however, and though we stayed out till nearly 9 P.M. we saw nothing.

The hunting parties arrived soon after we had finished dinner, and were enumerated. One small party of five still remained out, and of these particulars were obtained, and they were enumerated as not seen.

The return of the hunters was celebrated in the camp by an all-night revel, and dancing was still going on when the ship began to wake up at 5 A.M.

20th February.—We were rather late getting away in the morning, as we were taking with us some of the people of the camp for the coming expedition against the Jarawas, and after dancing all night it was not easy to get a move on them in the morning. However we got away at about 7 A.M., and an hour later met the S.L. "Sohrab" coming south to look for us, not having found us at our meeting place, Landfall Island, the previous evening.

Mr. Donald reported that there were no Andamanese on the east coast of the Islands, that is to say north of Havelock, except one small party which was at Port Cornwallis awaiting our arrival; I therefore decided to proceed to Cadell Bay, and anchor there for the night.

At about noon we were in the narrow passage between Trilby Island and North Andaman just south of Cadell bay, and here the Nancowry anchored, and the "Sohrab" came alongside to transfer to our bunkers some coal she was carrying on deck for us.

After tea we rowed round to Excelsior Island where we fished, and I had another try after turtle in an Andamanese canoe; but our luck was still out; we saw some, but could not get within spearing distance.

21st February.—We left the Trilby anchorage at 7 A.M., and arrived in Port Cornwallis at 8-30, where we found the party Mr. Donald had reported waiting for us. It consisted of one old man and three women, whom we enumerated. They were quite positive that there were no other Andamanese in the Port Cornwallis Basin, and as this confirmed the information I had from the other Andamanese I decided not to wait, but to push straight on to Stewart Sound.

We anchored in Stewart Sound, off Sound Island at about 12-30 P.M. and a little later Mr. Bonington came off, and I discussed with him, among other things, the arrangements necessary for the coming Census, and how best to enumerate the 600 or 700 coolies in his camps.

22nd February.—In the morning Mr. Bonington called for us in his motor boat, and we proceeded first to Curlew Island where I met Bora, the Andamanese sent across from the Interview Camp with the statement of the numbers in the camp. This he handed over. He said he had tried to get in touch with the independent parties on his way from Interview, but had failed to find them. This may or may not have been true. It is not easy to hit upon an Andamanese encampment which may be anywhere within an area of 100 square miles of trackless jungle, on the other hand Bora may have come straight through Austin Strait in his canoe, and made no attempt to find the camps.

Ten years ago it would have been easy to get in touch with outlying camps. It would have sufficed to sound the Syren once or twice, and the camps would have come in of themselves. With the establishment of the Forest Camps in Stewart Sound the voice of the Syren or steam whistle is a matter of daily occurrence, and carries no message for the Andamanese.

Bora was however quite prepared to give all necessary information to enable me to enumerate the absentees. He is one of the older generation, and was with me when I took the Census of 1911, and knew exactly what was wanted. The Andamanese has not in his own language any means of expressing a number greater than three, so that it is a little difficult for the Andamanese mind to wrestle with numbers which mount into double figures. However, remembering our methods at the last Census Bora demanded that I should write down at his dictation the names of the men in each of the missing parties. These he made me read over to him once or twice, and he consulted with his friends, and added a name now and then till all were satisfied that the list was complete. Then came the wives of such of the men as were married; then the children (alas lamentably few); and last of all the spinsters, widows and unattached females.

In this way I enumerated 42 persons. It was a long business, but I believe that the result was fairly accurate.

After this business was completed we proceeded with Mr. Bonington to visit the Base Camp on Austin Straits; a most interesting and informing trip.

On our return we rejoined the Nancowry, which had, in the meantime, come down the harbour, and was anchored alongside the jetty at Curlew Island, with a view to taking in water.

23rd February.—As I had no further use for the "Sohrab," and as I was a day ahead of my programme, I had sent the launch off on the 22nd to Long Island to warn them of my arrival, and to proceed from there to Port Blair without waiting for me.

We sailed ourselves at midnight, and by 6-30 A.M. were off Long Island. There we had to anchor for a couple of hours, waiting for the tide, and as soon as there was sufficient water on the bar we steamed up the Bamlungta creek to Sinkan, where we tied up alongside the jetty, and transferred ourselves and our belongings to trollies, and proceeded to Bomlungta camp arriving at the Rest House at about 1 P.M.

In the afternoon we trollied up to Kalsi Camp; but heavy rain prevented us from seeing very much there.

I saw Mr. O'Hara, and ascertained the progress made in the enumeration of the camps under his charge.

24th February.—In the early morning I visited the station and Hospital and also the Forest Office, where I looked through a number of the prepared schedule forms, and made notes of mistakes.

At 8 A.M. we started down the trolly line, arriving at Sinkan at about 9 A.M. where we went straight on board, and proceeded down the creek to Beehive, where we stopped to take in water and then sailed for Havelock.

It had come on to blow pretty fresh, and from the time we cleared the Islands we had a fairly rough trip, and there was a considerable sea running off the Havelock camp when we arrived there at about 3 P.M.

The Pahrewala came off and reported that all men and women were present in the camp, having been warned of our advent by the "Sohrab" on the previous day.

I decided to land after tea and enumerate the camp; but when the time came to go ashore I found that the Andamanese of our party had gone ashore in the big dug-out from the camp and not brought it off again. The Camp is situated inside a wide reef, and the tide being low it was not possible to land in a boat at this point, so to avoid a long row down the coast, and a walk up, I decided to go ashore in a small canoe we had on board. This proved however rather small for the state of the sea, and the load she had to carry, and it was soon apparent that the water was coming in quicker than it could be baled out with a nautilus shell; however it was better to go on than turn back, but we were still some 30 yards from the edge of the reef when the inevitable happened, and the canoe sank, and we had to swim the rest of the way.

I enumerated the camp and then returned to the Nancowry in safety in one of the big dug-outs belonging to the camp.

We sailed again at about 4-30 P.M., and after a somewhat rough passage arrived in harbour at about 8-15 P.M.

R. F. LOWIS,

Census Superintendent.

APPENDIX D.

Diary of Superintendent, Census Operations, of tour in the Andaman Islands.

SECOND CENSUS TOUR.

28th February 1921.—We went on board the S. S. Nancowry overnight, and she sailed at about 2 A.M.

At dawn we were off the Cinque Islands. At about 8 we crossed an extensive shoal with about three fathoms of water marked on it. There is a note on the chart that a shoal is reported in this vicinity, but its exact position is not marked. It is apparently a narrow shoal running for some distance east and west.

We were off North Brother by 9 A.M., and I decided to land and have a try for teal on the lagoon in the interior of the island. On shore we found an old Andamanese hut, and evidences of occupation, but old. It is probably a camp made by the Önges on one of their trips between Little Andaman and Rutland.

Making our way through the jungle, as we were nearing the edge of the lagoon we disturbed a flock of oceanic teal, evidently feeding in the jungle. Instead of flying up they ran for all the world like a covey of partridges into the dense tangle of vegetation fringing the lagoon, where we could not follow them.

Having found a way through the fringing tangle into the lagoon we found it to be nearly dry; though there were still about two feet of water at the lowest part; however, although we walked all round it, we saw only two cotton teal, one of which we shot. The oceanic teal were probably watching us from their strong strategical position in the impenetrable belt on the bank, from which they could not be dislodged without a dog.

On the way back to the boat we saw, or rather heard, large numbers of Hackle pigeon, and shot three.

After a bathe on shore, we returned to the Nancowry at about 11 A.M., and getting up the anchor steered for Bumila Creek in Little Andaman.

Arrived at the mouth of Bumila Creek, the water on the bar at the mouth looked rather shallow for the Nancowry, so we did not attempt to enter the creek as we had intended doing and stood on down the west coast in search of a quiet anchorage. About 2 miles down we came across the S. L. Bess anchored under the shelter of a reef, and joined her in what we found to be a very convenient anchorage.

The petty officer came off and reported that he had spent the previous night off Rutland, and had picked up, and brought away with him some Önges from the camps there. The Bess had arrived off Bumila Creek early in the day, and a party had rowed about 5 miles up the Creek in search of Önge encampments, but had found none.

There was an Önge hut on shore near where we were anchored, but it was deserted. The Önges from Rutland opined that the inhabitants must be inland hunting.

These Önges expressed ignorance of the numbers or location of the Önges further down the coast. They said it was not their country, and that if they trespassed there they would run risk of being shot; they were quite prepared however to accompany us there.

We landed after tea, and examined the deserted hut, and after a bathe returned to the ship for the night.

1st March.—Starting about 6-30 we steamed south down the coast accompanied by the Bess. After passing the mouth of Jackson Creek we saw some Andamanese on the shore, running along the beach. The Bess sent a boat off, but there was too much surf to permit of landing; however two of the men waded out over the reef and swam out to her, and they were brought on board the Nancowry.

These men reported that there was a hut on shore, and another in the jungle further north.

I decided to try and land and visit these places and we rowed inshore, but though we rowed about a mile up and down the coast we could not find a place where we could land on account of the surf, and the rocky nature of the shore. I therefore abandoned the attempt to land, and bringing the two local men off with me, as they were willing to accompany us, we returned to the ship. We had seen altogether 6 men and a boy, and ascertained the presence of two parties or units of population in that vicinity.

At about 9-30 we sighted two huts. The Bess sent a boat ashore and investigated, but reported that the huts were empty. The Önges opined that the inhabitants were inland hunting.

Whilst waiting here we anchored in 14 fathoms of water which was so clear that the bottom could be easily seen, and numbers of fish, including three or four large sharks, were observed swimming round.

The men we had picked up further north said that this was the limit of their country, and that the men further south were hostile to them.

Some miles further south we saw another hut. The Bess landed a party, who when they came off reported that the hut showed signs of occupation, with indications that the occupants had been in it the previous night; but whether it was deserted by chance or as the result of our approach it was impossible to say.

About an hour later we passed another hut, and two canoes on the shore. There was a heavy surf on the beach, but the Bess sent a boat off in the hope that contact might be made with those on shore. The boat however went too close in, and became involved in the surf, and swamped, and washed ashore, and all attempts on the part of the crew to launch her were of no avail. Eventually we had to send a boat to her assistance, which anchored out, and passed a line ashore, with the assistance of which the first was hauled out through the surf.

The shore party reported the huts empty, and as they had been on shore for nearly two hours, and it was obvious that no Önges could be expected there, we left the Bess to hoist her boat, of which two of the planks had been started, and pushed on in the hope of getting round to the south-east coast before dark.

Just as the sun was setting we found a suitable spot and anchored; the Bess joining us half an hour later.

Fish were plentiful and we caught a number. There was a hut on shore opposite the place where we anchored, but as we saw no Önges about we concluded that it, like the rest we had seen, was deserted.

2nd March.—There was some delay in getting under way, as we had to first take in water from the Bess. This operation was not complete till nearly eight; then the Bess sailed, and we followed as soon as our anchor was up.

As we were starting however we sighted some Andamanese on the shore about a mile north of the hut we had seen over night. The Bess with all the Andamanese of our party was already about two miles ahead. I hoisted the recall, and sounded the Syren, but though she hove to she made no attempt to return. She had as a matter of fact seen Andamanese too.

I decided to go ashore alone and see if I could induce the Önges to come off to the Nancowry; but when I got close in I found that the surf was too high to allow of landing except by swimming. The Önges in the meantime had come down to the beach. They were a family party and evidently desired to be friendly. I tried by signs to induce them to come out to the boat; but they held up a small baby as an excuse for not doing so. Eventually I returned to the ship and got some presents; tea, sugar, tobacco, a looking glass, etc., and rowed back to the shore. This time one of the men ventured to wade out and take the presents I had brought, and we parted the best of friends.

As I rowed off I saw the Bess coming south again, and some Andamanese running along the shore.

I left the Bess with more presents for the newcomers, and instructions to ascertain the numbers and composition of the second party, and myself proceeded north, as we had already wasted much valuable time.

We passed one hut in the south end of Hut Bay; but though we slowed down and whistled nothing showed, so we went on, knowing that if any Önges later appeared in answer to our whistle the Bess would see them.

This was the only hut we saw in Hut Bay, but as we were leaving the Bay we saw smoke rising from the jungle some distance inland, which may have been an Önge encampment, or possibly only a log burning in the jungle.

About 1 P.M. we passed another hut, apparently empty. The Bess had caught us up by this time, and we sent her to investigate, and proceeded ourselves up the coast.

Shortly after this we hooked a large "kokari" on the line towing astern; but after hauling it in, lost it through one of the men trying to gaff it. However a few minutes later we hooked the same fish or one exactly like it, which was safely hauled on board. It weighed about 35 lbs.

By this time we were off Labande Creek, near the mouth of which we saw a hut. The Bess was some distance astern, so I decided to land. Owing to shoal water the Nancowry had to anchor a long way out, making it rather a long pull in. We waited therefore till the Bess came.

up in the hopes that she would be able to tow us part of the way in ; but the water very soon got too shallow for her, and we had to row.

We found the hut empty, but showing signs of fairly recent occupation. We walked along the shore to the mouth of a small creek to the north of the hut. The Andamanese waded into the shoal water at the mouth of the creek, and began to shoot fish with their bows and arrows but were disturbed by the arrival, out of the creek, of a shoal of half grown sharks which cruised round, causing the Andamanese some excitement, and much amusement.

Rowing off to the ship I saw a Dugong close to the boat, but the Andamanese with the turtle spear were in the other boat.

The petty officer from the Bess reported that at the last place they stopped they found the hut empty ; but as they were rowing off a party of 12 Önges had appeared on the shore ; on their turning and rowing back however the Önges made off into the jungle and refused to come out. He also informed me that at our first stopping place he had seen and enumerated a party of 16 Önges in addition to the 15 I had seen.

On getting back to the Nancowry we started north again, and at about 3 P.M. passed another hut. It appeared to be empty, and as the landing looked bad I did not go ashore.

The navigation of this north-east corner of Little Andaman would be very dangerous for large ships as shoals are very numerous. We crossed one about 2 miles from the shore which appeared to extend for some distance out to sea. The soundings on the chart show nothing less than 9 fathoms in this vicinity ; whereas we got 3 to 3½ fathoms for some time.

We arrived at our anchorage of the night of the 28th February at about 5 P.M. We landed and bathed and I walked up the shore a little way, finding a temporary Andamanese camp which had been fairly recently occupied.

It is puzzling to find a temporary camp within half a mile of a permanent communal hut.

3rd March.—The Bess had been given instructions over night to return to Port Blair dropping the Önges at Rutland *en route*, and she sailed at about 2 A.M. We started about the same time for South Sentinel, and by 5 A.M. were off the island, and anchored soon after 6 on the north-west side.

South Sentinel is an uninhabited island, and on account of its isolated position is never visited by the Andamanese in their own canoes, and only at long intervals by parties from the settlement. Our object in going there was to give the Andamanese of our party the opportunity of getting turtle, which abound there, and to collect specimens of the great robber crab for the Calcutta Zoo and Museum. This crab is found only on this island of the group.

We landed at about 7 A.M., and within 5 minutes the Andamanese had speared and landed two large turtle, of which numbers were swimming along the shore. One of these was, with some trouble, hove into the boat and transferred to the ship ; the other was eventually released.

We spent about 2 hours on the island shooting pigeon, and collecting robber crabs, returning to the Nancowry at 9-30.

At 10 A.M. we sailed for Rutland, arriving in McPherson Straits by 4-30 P.M. We discovered the central Önge camp on the north side, not far from the old Chyria Tapu Forest camp.

I landed at once and found that the petty officer had all the men, women, and children collected in the camp, and I was able to enumerate them forthwith ; 61 in all. Afterwards we saw some dancing, and at dark returned to the Nancowry, the greater part of the camp accompanying us on board in their own canoes.

4th March.—We sailed from McPherson's Straits at about 4 A.M., and arrived in Port Blair at about 8 A.M.

R. F. LOWIS,

Superintendent, Census Operations.

APPENDIX F.

Diary of Superintendent, Census Operations of tour in the Nicobar Islands.

6th March.—Sailed in R. I. M. S. Minto (Captain Glanville, R.I.M.) at 3 P.M.

7th March.—Arrived off Car Nicobar about 10 A.M. and anchored in Sawi Bay.

The Agent came off and reported all well. He told me that he had completed the enumeration of the island; but that the schedules were not quite complete. He promised to hand them in on the return of the Minto to Car Nicobar on the 14th March.

I landed with Mr. Wilkinson and the rest of the party at about 2 P.M., and proceeded to the Agency, where I made over all papers to the agent, and looked through the schedules he had prepared. Later I visited the Elpanam and walked through Mus village, and returned to the Minto at about 6-30 P.M., after a bath on the Sawi Bay beach.

The Minto sailed at 8 P.M.

8th March.—Arrived off Chaura at 6-30 A.M. I landed with Mr. Wilkinson and Wazir Ali at 7-30. We explained the objects of our visit and proceeded to the north end of the village, or rather group of villages, and commenced the enumeration.

The natives quickly grasped what was required, and after enumerating a few houses, the party split up—I continuing to enumerate the houses southwards, and Messrs. Wilkinson and Wazir Ali proceeding to the southern end of the village and working northwards. Each party was accompanied by a couple of intelligent men of the Island who pointed out the inhabitants of each hut, and gave the names of such of the occupants who were for the moment absent. Working in this way the enumeration of the island was completed in about an hour's time. The total number of houses occupied, and the number of occupants showed a marked falling-off on the figures of last Census.

We returned to the Minto at about 9-30 A.M. and sailed at 10 for Nancowry after giving the usual presents for headmen.

Entry by Mr. Wilkinson.—

8th March.—The "Minto" arrived at Nancowry at 4 P.M. and I went ashore with Mr. Lowis and visited the agency; while he conducted the rest of the party to the cemetery, etc. The agent reported that he had had trouble with Pak, Headman of Trinkat, in the following manner.

Mewa Lal took Pak and some others over to Katchall in the sailing boat "Fairy Queen" on 24th February 1921. He left the boat at west bay and started off on foot for north bay, and left orders for the boat to follow with the above men. Mewa Lal walked about 15 miles to a village in north bay—; but the boat never came till dark—, and he was stranded for food. His cook finally brought the boat with two other men and reported as follows:

Pak had got drunk on Toddy after Mewa Lal left, and refused to take the boat on; one of the men with him named Ali gave the cook (Mahdaw) a hiding and the party was very obstructive. Mahdaw went out to the boat in a canoe with Ali, but the latter upset it, and Mahdaw had to swim ashore. He then asked Pak to follow him, but the latter refused, and said he didn't care for the agent. Mahdaw finally got two men, named Kawan and Kamlan and started off, leaving Pak, Ali and Samdo behind, all drunk. Kawan navigated the boat well in a strong breeze, and is recommended by the agent for a reward. Ali, Samdo, and Pak have not returned yet, and have run away, and are said to be threatening the agent, who is afraid of Pak. The latter has been twice warned and punished recently and does not appear fit to be a headman.

An earthquake shock was noticed from 12 midday to 12-2 P.M. on 5th March 1921. The people all ran out of their houses, and the shock was considerable.

The headman of Tapong on Trinkat found a bottle washed up—with a paper inside. This had been thrown over by an American Steamer *S. S. Suruga* (Barber Line) on January 2nd, 1921, 7 miles North East of Diamond Point, Sumatra—, and the finder was asked to send it to the address of the Steamer Company in New York, the idea was to assist the making of current charts. The agent however concluded the ship had been lost; I am "mailing" the paper to the address noted together with the position and date of finding.

A case of threatening to murder was reported from Dring. It appears that Narain Singh, a servant of the firm of L. Rati Lal (Mewa Lal's late father)— who is established at Dring— went to the house of a Nicobarese named Tanwal to ask for settlement of a debt, but Tanwal refused to come down and speak to him, as the dogs kept him from going up— he again asked the man to come down, but Tanwal said in his own language "Shuja Kachara" (I will kill him), and stood at the head of his steps in a threatening attitude. Narain Singh went away and wrote a letter to Mewa Lal reporting the case. The latter sent for the parties and examined them. Tanwal admitted the whole thing and pleaded that he had been told by a witch-doctor named Tulang of Bompoka that he would have to kill one trader, and that while he was arguing with Narain Singh he thought it would be a good opportunity to do it. He added that as he had failed to kill the traders, there was another Nicobarese left behind at Dring who would do the trick for him instead, but he refused to give the name of the man. The accused's wife was examined and also admitted that her husband had used the words "Shuja Kachara."

The man however denied it all when I tried him, though the woman admitted it. I am bringing Tanwal up to Port Blair, in the hopes of ridding him of the "devil".

I handed over papers and took over those which Mewa Lal gave me. Rs. 665-4 was taken from him, in Royalty fees, security deposits, trading licenses, etc.

We collected Tannamara, Ashlon, and a few others to help in the census—, Mewa Lal brought all his schedules of the central group on board, and himself accompanied us down to the Southern group.

I returned to the ship with the rest of the party at sunset and stayed the night.

9th March.—Started early next morning for Pulo Milo.

Mr. Lowis's Diary continued.

9th March.—Anchored in Pulo Milo anchorage at 11-30 A.M. It was arranged that I was to land on the north coast of Little Nicobar, and with the assistance of the Government Agent who had come with me, to enumerate the inhabitants of the villages on that coast, and, walking across the north east section of the island, enumerate the village or villages on the east coast.

In the meantime Mr. Wilkinson was to land on Pulo Milo and enumerate the villages on that island.

I landed as arranged and enumerated the small village to the south east of the anchorage and ascertained that there was only one village now on the east coast, within reach by road; and just as I was completing the work of enumeration the inhabitants of the said village arrived on their way to take part in certain festivities taking place at a village further to the West, so I was saved the walk.

Borrowing a canoe I returned to Pulo Milo where I landed and assisted in the taking of the census on that island, which work was speedily completed.

After bathing and shooting a few pigeon the party returned to the ship at dark.

10th.—The Minto sailed at daylight proceeding by way of the east coast of Little Nicobar to a point inside Menchal Island, where I put off in the whaler and sailed in shore to enumerate a village seen; the arrangement being for me to sail thence down the south coast of the island, enumerating all villages found there. There was a fair wind and the tide in our favour, and by 2 P.M. I had completed enumeration of all villages. These villages are very seldom visited and the inhabitants are not used to seeing strangers.

On the occasion of the last census in 1911, we found these villages, which only consist of a couple of huts each, deserted; and I wasnot surprised therefore as we approached the first to see the last of the inhabitants doing record time into the jungles.

We had with us a Nicobarese who knew the village well and was able to give me the names and all other necessary information regarding the inhabitants which numbered only 5.

The same thing happened at the next village, but here our guide could not help us. However we were confident of being able to get all required information regarding the inhabitants from Kondul, where we were spending the night.

The Minto had after dropping us in the morning proceeded down the straits between Great and Little Nicobars, and anchored to the south of Kondul Island. The wind was fair for the run across the straits, only a matter of about 5 miles, and I hoped to be on board again by 4 P.M. I knew the tide was running very strong from east to west and allowed about 1½ miles for drift, but found as time went on that this was not nearly enough, and I was unable to clear Kondul Island, and had eventually to beat up to pass it, and the tide setting us down, and the breeze falling, progress was very slow. At about 5, a squall came down from the east with heavy rain which caused us some inconvenience as we were without any sort of protection; but it got us home earlier than at one time seemed possible, and we reached the Minto by about 5-30 P.M. having been away about 8 hours.

Mr. Wilkinson was on shore on Kondul when we arrived on board, and he came off about dark having completed the enumeration of that island.

11th March.—We sailed from the Kondul anchorage at daylight and proceeded south for the enumeration of the villages on the west coast of Great Nicobar. This promised to be the most difficult operation of the whole trip. For one thing there is always a heavy surf on this shore which makes landing at all times difficult and sometimes dangerous. The coast is unsurveyed, and so infested with uncharted shoals that it is dangerous for a vessel to approach the shore. In fine weather it is possible, when the sun is high, to see shoal water at a considerable distance, and the danger is then less, but on the day in question the weather had broken. There was a very heavy swell, the sky was over cast, and heavy rain squalls were frequent; the land was often invisible, and the Commander of the Minto did not feel himself justified in approaching within 5 miles of the coast. It was arranged therefore that I was to proceed in shore in the motor boat, and then down the coast enumerating villages *en route*, and rejoin the Minto in the evening at Galatea Bay, a trip of about 25 miles.

It was obvious even from a distance of 5 miles that there was a heavy surf on shore, and as it was quite possible that I might find landing impossible; the Commander arranged to wait a couple of hours, so that if this was the case I could rejoin the ship without having to attempt the long run down the coast.

The weather was so thick that it was difficult to distinguish land marks on shore—, and we struck the coast some miles too far north, and had to proceed south before we found Pulo Babi the first inhabited point. Here we found an opening in the surf, and ran into a sheltered harbour with 3 Chinese Junks anchored in calm water. I landed with the agent and we proceeded to enumerate all huts found on shore. There has been a tendency in the past few years for the inhabitants of Great Nicobar to congregate at this point. The villages at Galatea Bay and other points have gradually disappeared, the inhabitants moving either to the Pulo Babi vicinity, or to one of the islands of Kondul or Pulo Milo. The reason for this is the fear they still seem to entertain of the Shom Pen in the interior. I tried to obtain information as to the number and distribution of the Shom Pen, but the headman could only tell me the approximate number of the tribe in the immediate vicinity of his village which he estimated at about 100; but what proportion this section was of the whole tribe he could not say.

We ascertained that the only other village in Great Nicobar was situated on Megapod Island about 10 miles south down the coast. This village is difficult of approach, and has not in consequence been visited for many years, and it is highly probable that the inhabitants would have run away if we attempted to land there.

Moreover it was getting late and it was imperative that we should get away as soon as possible. As therefore the headman was able to give me all information regarding the inhabitants of the village on Megapod Island, I enumerated them in this way, and we left for the Galatea Bay at about 3 P.M. in heavy rain.

We were all soaked to the skin by this time, and the Motor boat was without awning, and the run promised from the start to be a very unpleasant one. There was a very heavy swell, but otherwise no sea, and we made good progress. The tide was in our favour and at first it looked as if we would be in Galatea Bay in good time.

As we neared the south west corner of the island, it began to blow up, the swell began to be very high and steep, and our prospects of an uneventful voyage did not look so bright. By 4-30 it was blowing very strong, and we became involved in a very dangerous tide rip. At this moment the engine stopped and the driver announced that he could not restart it. It appeared that owing to the damp the engine was not running too well, and he had been using only petrol instead of the kerosine on which it was designed to run. The petrol was finished, and as the engine would not start on kerosine it was useless.

Our position was now very critical; we were on a lee shore, reef fringed, and with a surf on it through which no boat built could live. A lighter boat would have been ashore in 10 minutes, but the wind acted less strongly on the motor boat which is heavy, and has not over much free board, and we had time to step the mast and set the sail, an operation of some difficulty in the sea then running. The wind blew diagonally to the coast and it was not possible to continue in the direction of Galatea Bay. In fact the size and position of the sail in the boat made sailing in any direction except that of the wind very difficult. Very slowly we got the boat heading up the coast in the direction from which we had come, but the best course she would sail on would not have carried her clear of the surf, so we lowered the sail and took to the oars. The boat was so heavy that the 6 oars which was all we could muster made very little impression. However we soon discovered that the tide was carrying us very quickly down the coast in the right direction. The wind having fallen the sea had gone down somewhat, and things generally looked more cheerful.

A little later we made out the smoke of a steamer on the horizon standing north far out to sea, and presently were able to make out that it was the Minto.

What had happened was that she had looked in at Galatea Bay and not finding us there, and not liking the look of the anchorage in the weather prevailing, had determined to spend the night at sea believing that we had not attempted the journey round the coast, and were probably lying either at Pulo Babi, or under Megapod Island, where she hoped to find us in the morning.

We hoisted a flag on a bamboo without attracting her attention as it was growing dark, and we did not show up clearly against the land; but when hoisted the sail, the direction of the wind being now favourable she saw us and altered course.

We were too close in shore for her to come to our assistance, and as a matter of fact with wind and tide in our favour, and the sea very much less we were all right, and we arrived alongside about 7 P.M. very relieved to have come safely out of a very hazardous situation.

Any one who has had experience of the surf on the west coast of Great Nicobar when the swell is running high will realize how slender would have been our chances of making a safe landing had we been driven ashore.

12th March.—The Minto sailed next morning before daylight. We had intended spending the day in Galatea Bay and exploring the Galatea river in the hopes of seeing something of the Shom Pen ; but the weather being so uncertain, and the state of the sea such that it was practically certain that the surf on the bar would make it impossible for a boat to get into the river, we reluctantly gave up the idea.

About 7 A.M. we passed the wreck of the Fazulka, but did not stop to visit her, viewed through glasses she appeared to have altered her position very little in the past year, but was somewhat lower in the water, and had taken a decided list.

The weather was much clearer, but there was still rain about. We had a quiet trip and anchored in Nancowry harbour for the night at 4-30 P.M.

13th March.—We spent the day in the harbour. I took over all census schedules from the Assistant Agent, and settled all outstanding matters.

Parties landed on the Nancowry and Malacca sides of the harbour for shooting and bathing.

The Minto sailed at 3-30 P.M.

14th March.—Anchored in Sawi Bay at about 9 A.M. Landed after breakfast and proceeded to the Agency with Mr. Wilkinson. I took over money orders and telegrams from traders whilst Mr. Wilkinson counted and took over Cash from the Agent.

After completing this work I went for a walk with the agent through the village, and took some photos, and then proceeded to the beach. The whaler came off for us at 1 P.M. and the Minto sailed as soon as the anchor was up.

15th March.—Arrived in Port Blair at 10 A.M.

R. F. LOWIS,

Dated 18th March 1921. *Deputy Commissioner, Port Blair.*

APPENDIX. G.

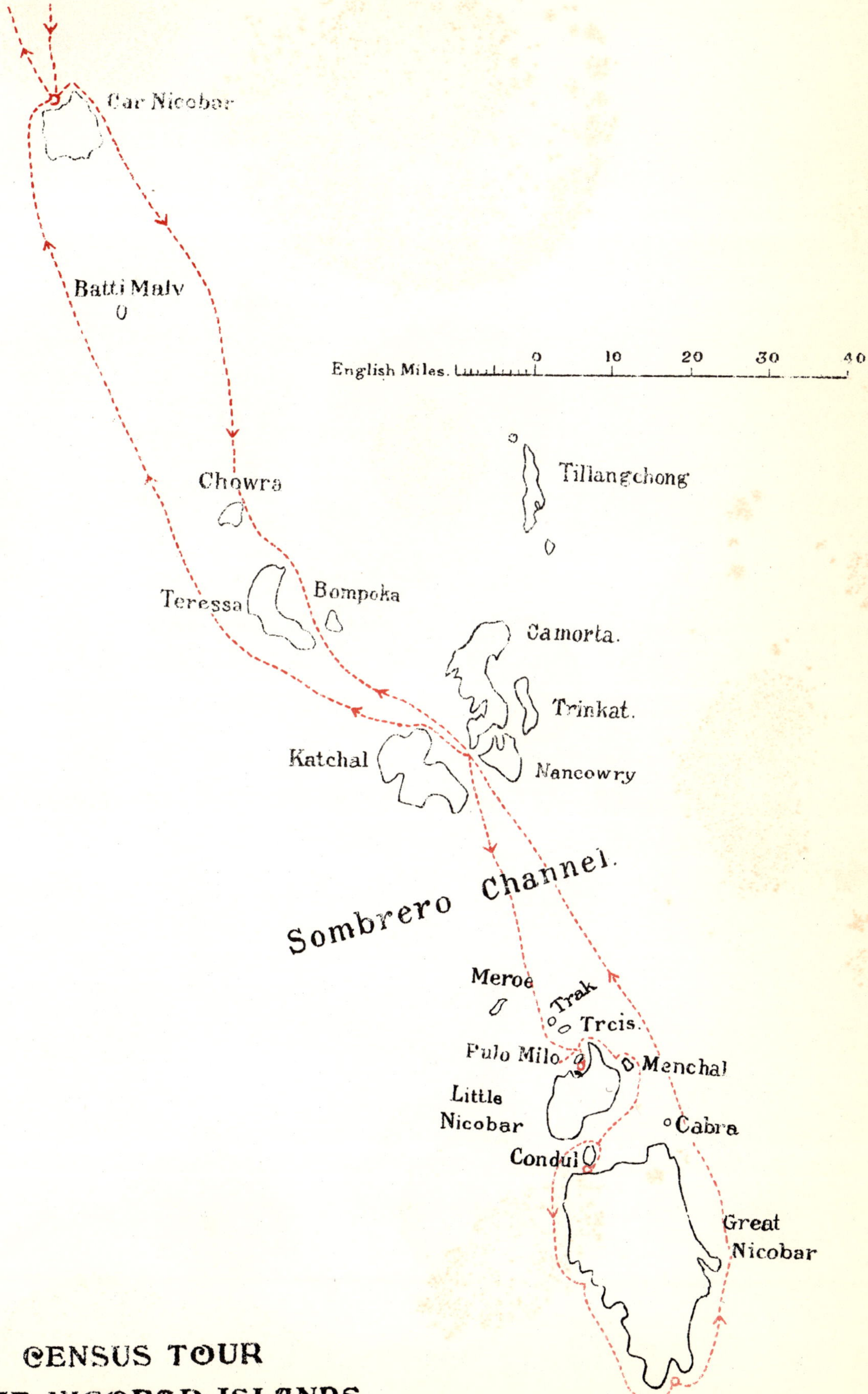

CENSUS TOUR
IN THE NICOBAR ISLANDS.

APPENDIX H.

Extract from report of Mr. Morgan's expedition against the Jarawas in March 1918.

My party consisted of myself, 12 Andamanese, 16 Police, and 35 coolies. We left Port Blair on the 23rd February, 1918 and arrived at Port Campbell on the 25th February. I had intended to disembark on the east side of Port Campbell, but owing to the inability of the "Nancowry" to get anywhere near the shore—(she ran aground near Clyde Island)—I was forced to land, and pitch my base camp on the stretch of sand just close to Dalrymple Reach.

On the 26th February, I sent Havildar Jai Singh to explore in a southerly direction, and myself went in a south-westerly direction (*vide* the map).

Havildar Jai Singh returned at sunset, and reported that at the point marked A on the map, he had found :—

(1) the fresh foot-prints on the sand of two Indians and about 9 Jarawas,

(2) some freshly burnt leaves,

(3) some freshly cut branches, and

(4) marks of children playing on the sand.

Next morning I started to follow up the clues. The tracks were exactly as Havildar Jai Singh had described. At one point it was clear that a Jarawa father had been fishing from a tree over-hanging the high tide, while his children had been playing on the sand nearby. There were the remains of a fire. A little further on, on the sand, were the foot-prints of several more Jarawas, and of at least one man whose feet were larger than my own. These tracks led to the mouth of the "Kharee," and were joined there by the tracks of more Jarawas coming from the opposite direction. It was clear that a large party of Jarawas had come down from the hill to fish there the previous day, and had returned in the afternoon.

We followed these tracks for several miles up various nullahs. Wherever we found Jarawa footmarks, we also found the larger footmarks. There were no old villages, probably on account of the scarcity of water. At 4-0 P.M. it was getting dark, and as there appeared to be no prospect of reaching the Jarawas before sunset, we took advantage of a pool of stagnant water, and halted for the night. As it happened, had our trackers gone on another ½ of a mile, the exact position of the Jarawa village would have been discovered, and we could have killed them all early next morning.

At 7-0 A.M. we pushed on. At 7-30 A.M. we came across a pool of running water, and almost immediately afterwards we heard the Jarawas ahead of us. The Andamanese fell back, and with 5 sepoys I crept along the nullah. Before we came within killing distance, the Jarawas heard us and raised the alarm. One of these voices was peculiarly like the voice of an Indian. We rushed towards the village. Abandoning everything the Jarawas fled headlong into the jungle. I saw an unclothed woman with her child—a Jarawa youth with red cloth round him and a full-grown Jarawa. I put 2 barrels of buck shot into the last at about 15 yards distance. He dropped his bow and arrows, but slipped into the jungle. Sepoy Kirpa wounded a Jarawa with buck shot at close range.

The men behind were armed with rifles—I do not think that they hit anybody. There was a great deal of blood in the nullah, and the Andamanese followed this for some miles. They then came to a running stream and some thick jungle, and the track was lost.

The village consisted of 10 huts, inhabited by 20 to 30 Jarawas. Each hut was about 3 feet high and 6 feet square. The diameter of the village was about 20 yards. There was thick jungle on all sides, a small nullah running down one side.

I attach a photograph of the village :—

We brought away a large number of bows, arrows, and utensils, and burnt everything else.

We then returned to our base-camp.

Next day, 1st March, I moved my base-camp to Ike Bay. I took out a search party in the evening, and found an old Jarawa village and track not far off. I followed up this track for about two miles, and after satisfying myself that we were out of ear-shot of any Jarawas, returned to camp. Next morning, we marched eastwards along a Jarawa main road. We passed several old villages—with an average of 10 huts each,—and, finally, about noon, reached the top of the middle range. There we found a freshly built communal hut. It was empty at the time, but was clearly in regular use.

There were Jarawa paths leading to this hut from all directions. We followed one in a north-westerly direction (*vide* the map). At the point marked Q we heard a Jarawa felling a tree about ½ a mile ahead. The Andamanese said the village must be close by. As it was now about 4-0 P.M. and getting dark, I decided to halt for the night, and attack the village in the early morning. At 3-30 A.M. next morning we started up the nullah. We followed various tracks without success till 7·0 A.M. At noon we returned to the communal hut—burnt it—and reached our base-camp at sunset.

Next day we explored the east beach of Port Campbell, and Petrie, and Defence Islands. We found no traces of Jarawas. On the 5th March, we went south-eastwards (*vide* the map). At the summit of the range there were old Jarawa villages. We then went southwards for 7 miles down a long nullah (not marked in the printed map), towards Pulon Jig.

This nullah is evidently a favourite haunt of the Jarawas in the rains. We passed 15 old villages. Each village had from 10-15 huts. Unfortunately none of them were inhabited, and we did not find anything worth destroying until we reached the point marked C on the map. Here we found another communal hut similar to the one destroyed two days previously.

After destroying it we returned to camp. On my arrival at sunset, I found that sepoy Surjan,—one of the five camp guards, had been shot dead at noon, within 10 yards of the camp, by some Jarawas who had been prowling round. He had left the camp to ease himself.

NOTES.

The presence of runaways with the Jarawas.

Among the fresh Jarawa foot-prints discovered on the north of sandy islands on the 26th February,—and thence right up to the Jarawa village,—were the large foot-prints of at least one man (probably more), who is not an aboriginal. At the moment when the Jarawas were surprised by our attack on the 28th February, I heard distinctly the shouts of a Burmese or an Indian. In my opinion at least one of the band which we tracked and surprised is not an aboriginal, but a native of India.

2. The responsibility for the recent raids on the settlement.

Among the articles which I sent to the Deputy Commissioner for identification on the 29th February, were an iron file, 4 degchis, nails, an enamel cup, a piece of khaki cloth, a large number of iron implements, and two katoras numbered with convict numbers. The result of the identification will show whether this gang of Jarawas was concerned in the raids on Templegunje and the Forest Department. It is the Templegunje villagers who have always asserted that there is a runaway with the Jarawas.

3. Jarawa Census.

I came across over 20 old Jarawa villages. Each village had between 7-15 huts. The jungle is full of well beaten Jarawa tracks. Each of the two communal huts which we destroyed was capable of holding 100 persons. There were several women and children in the village which we raided on the 28th February. Wherever we found grown-up Jarawa foot-prints we also found the foot-prints of their children. We recovered a large number of nets and small bows. The nets are made by the Jarawa women, and the small bows are used by the children.

In my opinion the number of Jarawas is considerably larger than has up to the present been supposed.

4. Water is extremely scarce on the western slopes. On a similar expedition every cooly should be provided with a water bottle.

5. On account of the thickness of the jungle it is usually necessary to get within 20 yards of the Jarawas in order to kill them. It is difficult for a party of police to do this without being discovered. It would not be difficult for a party of Burmans and Andamanese. 30 Burmans armed with guns and daos, with some Andamanese to track for them would wipe out every Jarawa in the place in 2 or 3 years.

(Sd.) D. L. MORGAN.

7th March 1918.

NOTE.

Mr. Morgan's report does not help us very much in estimating the numbers of the Jarawa tribe; but it is of great value in helping us to settle other vexed questions.

In the Jarawa raids of 1917, which were of an extraordinarily daring character, there was some suspicion that the men responsible were not Jarawas at all, but members of the so-called friendly tribes.

The evidence on which the rumours were based was that the raiders were wearing red langotis, and could speak a few words of Hindustani; whereas, so far as was then known, the Jarawas always went quite naked, and never having had communication with the settlement could have no knowledge of any language but their own. There were therefore some grounds for suspecting that the raids were the work of disaffected Andamanese of the friendly tribes, who were, it was suggested discontented with the policy of keeping them, so far as possible, away from the debasing influences of the settlement.

Those who know the Andamanese best did not credit the theory ; but there is no doubt that it received wide acceptance.

It was more particularly in regard to the raids in the vicinity of the villages of Templegunje and Manpur that the rumours were most persistent.

The evidence collected by Mr. Morgan in the course of his expedition is of the greatest value in disproving the above theory. The articles found in the Jarawa camp raided proved beyond doubt that the occupants were responsible for the attacks on Templegunje and Manpur. Further he saw a Jarawa wearing a red langoti ; and there was strong evidence that the camp he attacked had at least one Burman or native of India in it. The presence of such a man, presumably an escaped convict, among the Jarawas would explain their having a smattering of Hindustani, and would also account for their wearing langotis.

Recently an escaped convict, recaptured after being at large for nearly a year, claimed to have been a prisoner in a Jarawa encampment for some months. Cross examination proved that the greater part of his story was pure fabrication ; but there may have been a slight substratum of truth in it ; for it has since transpired that he was a member of a gang of Burman runaways who had a well founded and appointed hut in the outskirts of the Jarawa country, in which some of the occupants are supposed to have maintained themselves for a couple of years. This encampment was discovered by the members of one of the columns of this year's Jarawa expedition, and one of the occupants captured. This man claims that he has seen Jarawas and given them food . This is very possibly true, as it is hard to believe that they could have existed for so long in the Jarawa country unless they were on moderately friendly terms with the tribe.

R. F. LOWIS.

APPENDIX I.

Extract from Mr. Field's report on the Jarawa raid on the cane file at Chilan-jai.

On Saturday, October 30th, at about 6 A.M. the cane file consisting of 22 convicts, and 2 petty officers were cooking food preparatory to starting out for the day's work. Without any warning a party of men, estimated by the convicts at twelve in number, came out of the jungle right up to the hut, and at a distance of about six yards shot three convicts as they were lying in their beds. Two never moved ; the third managed to run about ten yards and then dropped dead. In the meantime the rest of the file fled, though five of them were wounded before they finally escaped. The convicts say that many more of them would have been killed or wounded but that their dogs created a diversion by attacking the assailants, one of whom at least was bitten before the dogs were killed or driven off.

All who escaped fled into the jungle ; some made their way over the hills to Go-pla-ka-bang, others followed the coast to North Bay.

Their assailants looted the place and cleared off with all the iron, and a good deal of the clothes, blankets, etc.

The above is the story as I had it from the wounded and other survivors on the day after the raid.

The question at once arises as to who were the assailants. When examined by me convicts all asserted that they had been attacked by ordinary " janglies " (*i.e.*, Andamanese of the Settlement Homes), and nothing could shake their view. They said some wore red, and some wore white loin cloths, and some had clay plastered on their foreheads. They were positive that they were not Jarawas. Two or three of them said that they could identify one of their assailants if confronted with him.

All this is very vague, and I doubt if any definite conclusion can ever be arrived at. Personally I have no experience in a matter like this, and can hardly offer an opinion at all. It is a fact that on the Sunday preceding this raid a Jarawa fire was seen from Go-pla-ka-bang on the hills opposite, at about 7 P.M. This shows clearly that Jarawas were in the vicinity. From where the fire was seen to Chilan-jai is about four miles over the hills.

Since the occurrence various rumours have been afloat to prove that these assailants were ordinary janglies, and not Jarawas ; but no definite piece of evidence has been brought to light to prove this statement.

C. G. FIELD,
D. O. W. G.

9th November 1920.

N.B. Two of the wounded men have since died of their wounds.

NOTE.

It is extraordinary now this theory that the friendly Andamanese are responsible for these raids, persists in the face of proof to the contrary. In the above account of the occurrence there is not one shred of evidence to show that the raid was not the work of Jarawas, and plenty to show that it was.

To the average person the Jarawa is exactly like any other Andamanese, all Andamanese smear their heads on occasion with clay, and Mr. Morgan's report on his expedition against the Jarawas in 1918 proves that they now wear " langotis." The only other evidence in favour of the Jarawas is that the raid was carried out at a spot about four miles outside what is generally looked upon as the boundary of their territory ; this boundary is a purely arbitrary one fixed by ourselves, and is probably unknown to the Jarawas themselves, the sphere of whose operations is restricted only by considerations of their own convenience and safety. The fact that Jarawas were known to be in the vicinity a few days previously seems to me to complete the case against them.

If further proof of the innocence of the friendlies is necessary it is furnished in the census returns herewith published. The evidence shows that this particular raid was carried out by a party of not less than twelve men. Now the raid could not possibly have been the work of men of the Yerewas, the northern group of tribes ; their most southerly camps are at Stewart Sound, and it would be impossible for a large party of them to come 80 to 100 miles south without our knowledge or assistance. It must therefore have been the work of members of the Bojigngiji, or southern group. The census returns show that there were at the time exactly 12 adult males of this group. Of these one or two are generally in hospital, others are old feeble and decrepit and apart from the fact that the whereabouts of the majority is generally well known it would be impossible to collect a party of twelve men from the Andamanese in the south capable of carrying out an operation of this kind.

R. F. LOWIS,
Superintendent, Census Operations.

15th April 1921.

APPENDIX J.

Report of Officer Commanding, Column II, of Jarawa Expedition, March 1921.

6th March 1921.—Left Bamboo Flat at 9-30 A.M. accompanied by Mr. Baines, a party of 15 Police, six Andamanese and 40 convicts. Anchored in Shoal Bay creek opposite the Gobang branch at 3 P.M. The whole party landed and a base camp formed about four miles up the Miletilek creek by 9 P.M.

7th March 1921.—Sent out a scouting party of six Andamanese and three Burmans. Discovered a good water supply about a mile north of the camp. The scouting party returned at 3 P.M. and reported that they had come across two days old encampment of about eight Jarawas, who were out on a fishing expedition along the Jirka-tang creek.

8th March 1921.—Set off at 7 A.M. with eight Police, 20 convicts and five Andamanese in a north-westerly direction. At 9-30 A.M. we suddenly came on a big camp half way down a hill and at the head of a fresh water nullah. The camp was empty, but according to the Andamanese it had been occupied about three or four days previously. We spent half an hour there collecting any material we could find. There were 20 huts, small leaf affairs, each occupied by two people. Among the things found was an old strip of cloth with the blue convict stripe on it. This was the only evidence procurable to show these particular Jarawas had been engaged in any of the recent raids on the settlement. No traces were found to indicate that there were any runaways living with them. From this camp two well defined paths led one northwards towards the creek, and the other south-wards towards Gobang. As this party of Jarawas had gone northwards we followed after them. At 2-30 P.M. we came down to the creek after very hard marching through the densest jungle. I decided it was time to look for fresh water, and a suitable place to camp. We followed the creek for about a mile until we came to a place where a small nullah branched off. My three leading Burmans and one Andamanese went up this nullah to see if there was any fresh water there, while the rest of the party halted, Mr. Baines, the Sub-Assistant Surgeon and myself were seated within five yards of each other, the convict porters altogether slightly behind us, and the police as usual when a halt was made all round. The Burmans had hardly been gone five minutes, when we heard a cry of " Banduq lao " Mr. Baines and I jumped up with the intention of taking the Police forward as fast as we could, when the Sub-Assistant Surgeon lost his head and fired his shot gun into the air. Immediately after the police Havildar also fired, it appears that the Sub-Assistant Surgeon realised that Jarawas were coming, and in order to frighten them fired. The Police Havildar hearing one shot fired from near where Mr. Baines and I had been seated, and realising that the Jarawas were somewhere about thought that I had given orders to fire.

By the time I had found out the real reason of these two shots being fired, and had prevented further firing; the Burmans had rejoined our party in a considerable state of excitement. It appears that they had run into a party of 8 or 9 Jarawas about 200 yards up the nullah. The Jarawas had jumped up and pursued them; and were close behind them rapidly approaching our main party when the two shots were fired; at once they turned about and fled. By the time we reached the spot where the Burmans had first seen them there was no trace of them; nor could our Andamanese pick up any definite track; as the jungle they had taken to was hard and leaf strewn. After casting round for about three quarters or an hour or so, we decided that nothing more could be done, as it was then about 4 P.M. and our porters were about tired out. In fact it was felt to be useless trying to run down this particular party now that they knew we were armed with firearms. The whole expedition had been in vain.

9th March 1921.—It was decided to try our luck the other side of the Cholunga ridge, as all the Jarawas in the Mitetilek-Jirka tang area would be in hiding, and could never be tracked. At about noon after a stiff climb over the ridge we struck the Pulom-jig stream. We decided to camp there; while I took two police and two Andamanese and worked up stream and Mr. Baines with a similar party worked down. We both returned about 3 P.M. having seen a few old traces, but nothing in the shape of a hut or encampment to lead us to suppose they were anywhere near.

10th March 1921.—As our Burman guides told us it would take us two days to get back to our base camp, we decided to start back that morning as there seemed no likelihood of coming across Jarawas where we were. By starting at 6 A.M. and marching continuously, we managed to reach our base camp at 2 P.M. all pretty tired. On our way we came across the remains of a communal hut about two years old, near the top of the western slope of the ridge.

11th March 1921.—Sent off a message to headquarters asking for orders to return. Mr. Baines, myself, two police and an Andamanese rowed up Jirka-tang creek in the hopes of catching some of the Jarawas fishing. We failed to do so, however, though there were plenty of fresh traces of their having been there.

Returned to launch at 3 P.M., and made arrangements to break up the camp and return to Port Blair the next day.

The Police were sent to destroy the encampment, which they successfully accomplished.

12th March 1921.—Orders received to return. Left Mr. Baines in-charge and returned overland to Wimberley Gunj.

GENERAL REMARKS.

1. The party was too large. Six guns with the main party and four more if a base camp is to be formed, is in my opinion sufficient. There is no chance of a stand-up fight as has been proved time and again. Once a single shot has been fired no Jarawas will be seen again. The only chance is to take them by surprise, and come on them unexpectedly, before they know any armed party is after them.

2. No traces of any runaways, being in this particular camp were found. Had there been we should have been certain to have seen his foot-prints somewhere round about the camp.

3. The only evidence that this party of Jarawas had participated in any of the recent raids on the settlement was a narrow strip of cloth about an inch wide with the blue convict stripe on it, found lying in front of one of the huts.

4. The Burmans were invaluable in the jungle in clearing the way and in finding their way about. I am reporting on these to the Deputy Commissioner. Three Andamanese from the Port Blair settlement were useful in picking up the tracks, and pointed out the signs, etc. The two from Kalapahar and the fat man whom nobody could talk to or understand and who was said to be a Jarawa, were of no use.

G. G. FIELD.

APPENDIX K.

Rough notes made by the Revd. W. R Park, C.I.E., regarding a festival, a part of which was witnessed by him of the village of Lapati, Car Nicobar, on the 1st of March 1915.

I visited Lapati on the afternoon of March 1st and found about 2,000 natives gathered together for the festival. It was a festival that had begun the previous evening, and would be finished the night I was there. The moon was at the full.

The main idea that seemed to underlie the ceremonies was that a great evil fish was about to emerge from the sand of the sea-shore, and do a great deal of harm among the people. The natives professed that they did not understand the full meaning of the ceremony ; but carried it out as it was a very old custom and superstition.

When I arrived at 1 P.M., a portion of the sea shore had been marked off, in length about 500 yards. I was told it would be contrary to custom, and " sin ", for me to walk between these marks and the sea.

As I watched branches of cocoanut palms were cut down and tied to stakes already driven into the ground, and thus a rough fence about 3 feet 6 inches high was made of the length above mentioned. Next pieces of cloth were unrolled, each some 40 feet by 3 feet 6 inches, and held up against this fence. Then throughout its length fringes of beads were unrolled from sticks, and likewise held up by willing hands at the upper part of the cloth. This part of the work was done chiefly under the direction of the middle aged women, who displayed great energy and excitement. As the festival is only held once in 15 or 20 years the younger generation did not know what part to take, and had to be instructed.

The fence had now assumed the appearance of a great drag-net, and it had been erected to prevent the " great evil fish " from passing by when it should emerge from the ground.

Incidentally I may mention that it was quite obvious that the women seemed under the impression that they would receive good fortune through holding up the net, probably in the way of giving birth to more children.

The enclosed space was now entered by about twenty men, each with some kind of hat upon his head , (either a very old straw hat, naval cap, bowler, or old silk top hat), and a fringe of green paper round his neck ; this being in addition to the usual full dress costume that consists of a piece of red tape round the waist. First three plaited fish-shaped mats, made of leaves, and representing an octopus, a lobster, and some more ordinary fish, were dragged over the sand of the enclosure from one end to the other. Next baskets of the fruit of some overhanging trees were given to the men by an old woman, who struggled hard with another woman for the honour of doing this service. This fruit is about half the size of a cocoanut, and is ordinarily used for poisoning the water for the purpose of killing fish. Then two men entered with long and sharp pointed stakes. After carefully inspecting the sand for some minutes one of them suddenly thrust his stake into the sand with considerable vigour, and the other doing the same, they appeared to be engaged in slaying some monstrous unseen fish.

This same performance was carried out again by other men at the other end of the enclosure. The poison fruit was buried in the holes thus made.

As this point of the procedure I was informed that at the last festival of this kind, which had taken place from 15 to 20 years earlier (the Nicobarese chronology is vague), a male devil had been previously caught and was buried in the sand. This time they had managed to obtain a female devil which they were going to bury to keep the male company. What it consisted of I could not ascertain. The only information given was that it was wrapped up carefully in leaves, and until I left the place the ceremony could not proceed, for it was not the custom to allow an outsider to remain longer. Accordingly as it was the natives wish, and only one hour remained before the station steamer was to leave the island, I hurried away.

One other point in connection with the feast was mentioned to me : the Nicobarese supposed that a process of generation had been going on within the earth during the past 14 years, and that for the next seven years this process would cease, and no creation would be in progress ; consequently the coming years would not be so plentiful as the past, and unless the creative power is renewed at the end of seven years a great famine will ensue.

There was no dancing after the festival, but all returned to their respective huts, where large stores of food and water had been laid up. They would not leave their compounds for the next seven days and seven nights, because they feared misfortune in the form of treading on poisonous fish-bones in that period of time.

PORT BLAIR, W. R. PARK,
3rd March 1915. *Chaplain.*

APPENDIX L.

Extract from Diary of Mr. E. Hart, Government Agent, Car Nicobar.

The quaint customs of the Nicobarese have been described by many visitors, and do not call for comment here. In the devil-driving ceremony this year I noticed that the " Menluanas " had seven or eight sword bayonets, the latter brass handled, the former the old triangular affairs. None were sharp enough to cut, though a thrust might give a nasty wound.

I am assured that the bayonets were most effective in driving out the devils.

On June 12th Davidson's mother was buried in great state. She is said to have been nearly 100 years old.

The grave was dug in "El-panam" in the coral rock, about 3 feet deep.

"All the world" (ta-Kok-haroo-tarik) was invited, and two hundred came.

The ceremony resembled a Burmese "pongyi byan" in some respects. There was the dragging to and fro of the coffin, only in this case it was in a big racing canoe (arp assolo). It was dragged around the village by teams of men pulling on canes a hundred feet long. Some made a pretence of dragging it backwards, but it never went backwards, only it was held still for a few minutes. It was a tug of war with a coffin for the mark. Women lay on the coffin and howled.

The coffin was put into the grave, and a dozen fowls, and three little pigs were stabbed all over and flung in with it. Then it was covered over. It was ghastly.

The canoe, a fine big affair, was chopped and sawn to bits and laid up under the dead-house.

Five big pigs were tied up under the dead-house during the ceremony—"to please the spirits"—; but at dusk they were quietly set free and driven away into the jungle.

The company took lumps of meat from the funeral feast, about a thousand pounds weight of pork, and dispersed. They declared that it was, "lork-ta-gor", *i.e.*, a grand burying.

All the usual ceremonies of sweeping the spirits out of the grave, etc., were duly performed, and a fine grave post has been set up.

APPENDIX M.

The Ossuary Feast on Car Nicobar.

The Ossuary Feast is probably the most important of the numerous religious events of the Nicobarese year. Not that the feast is an annual one, for it is not; there is no fixed date for its observance, which depends on the ability of the village to furnish the not inconsiderable material necessary for the proper performance of the ceremony. In bad times the intervals are of longer duration than when the people are prosperous; but as each village invites the inhabitants of surrounding villages to their own particular feast the Nicobarese have fairly frequent opportunities of enjoying themselves in this fashion.

I have obtained from the Rev. G. Whitehead, who was for some years in charge of the S. P. G. Mission on Car Nicobar, an excellent account of this festival, which on account of its accuracy and conciseness I venture to reproduce, although an account of this feast has already appeared in a previous report.

R. F. L.

The Ossuary Feast.

(*Or more literally "The Festival of the eating of Pork".*)

Some two or three years after the death of some one, and indeed every two or three years; for the festival is one which calls for co-operation on the part of the whole village, they hold a council of Elders of the village to consider the question of keeping, that year, the Ossuary Feast. If all agree, and are able to contribute, pigs having become numerous again, they fix a day for the setting up of a post with food for the dead hanging on it.

Then they cut down and trim a slender straight tree, of about the height of a cocoanut palm, and this is carried to the village. They chisel through this post, and put in pegs on which the food is to be tied. Then when everything is ready it is erected, without the aid of pulleys. The post is put into its hole, and fastened in position with long pieces of cane, such as are used for the rigging of their canoes.

The food for the dead is strung together, and a man goes up the post, and ties the food on to the pegs of the post. He takes with him a long thin rope (not cane) tied in a loop, and passes it over one of the pegs. Another man stands at the foot of the post also keeping hold of the rope, and the food is placed in baskets and hoisted up, yams of different kinds, pandanus (or bread fruit), and ripe cocoanuts, also pieces of pork in baskets, and thus tied on to the pegs of the post as offerings to the dead. The post with the food on it is left standing until the Ossuary Festival. Then, one month before the festival, the people of the place where the feast is to be held (more literally "of those who wish to eat pork") severally go to their friends in the other villages to tell them about the feast (literally "that they wish to eat pork").

Next month when the time for the feast is getting near, they prepare pens for the pigs, one pen for each pig. Then on the ninth day of the month they go again to invite their friends who live in the other villages. "On the day after tomorrow" say the messengers, "will be the decoration of the houses", (*i.e.*, inside, with a great display of cloth, plated spoons, forks, etc.), on the third day the pigs will be put into the pens, and on the fourth day they will be slaughtered.

Some of the invited guests will come on the day of the decoration of the houses ; and these will help by bringing in the pigs from the jungle, beginning with those nearest the village. The hosts (*i.e.*, the whole population of the village where the feast is held) are busy with other preparations. The pig is generally caught by laying hold of its outer fore leg, and thus throwing it over, whilst someone is feeding it, and shading its eyes with the spathe of the areca palm ; but the more timid or wildish ones are caught with a noose or crook.

The people then go to the village, carrying the pigs round to all the various groups of houses, singing the songs they have made in " praise of the pig ", or rather about the pigs, and their success or failure in catching them ; or about the other incidents of the feast. Wherever they go betel nut and cigarettes are served out to the carriers, who having gone the round of the village, return to the house of the owner of the pig, and put it into its pen, and then wait a bit for their comrades who may not yet have come in with the pigs from the more distant plantations.

After that all the visitors prepare for the dance ; for not until after the bones have been exhumed do the people of the village dance, they are too busy ; but only the guests. The women dance first by themselves. The dancing must be kept up all night long, at least in the group of houses where the post with food for the dead on it has been erected ; sometimes however if a village is very poor, no post has been erected.

When the messengers go round to give notice of the feast, they especially invite those skilled in dancing ; and if any village is not disqualified (by sickness or recent deaths) for dancing, a troupe will have practiced at home, sometimes a new dance and song, so that they may acquit themselves with credit before the whole island.

Perhaps there may be a dozen long pieces, and four or five short ones in a set. They begin with the short pieces, and then after each long piece (excepting the last) they sing and dance the short pieces over again. Also at the end of each long piece there may be a song (with dance), partly at least, in English, Burmese or Hindustani.

Next morning they cut down the lofty post of the food of the dead, and it is thrown away in the jungle, together with the food tied on it ; then a pig is killed as a special " offering ", the pole of its pen being chopped to get it out. People eat most of the flesh ; but some of it has a string passed through it, and it is put on the " offering (sic)" together with the intestines. The offering is laid on some green cocoanut leaves torn into ribbons, and on which the blood of the food of the offering has been sprinkled, at the very place where the post had stood.

After this most of the pigs are taken out of their pens and killed. The pigs are singed, and more or less roasted somewhere near the village, and cut up into pieces, and pork is then given to all the visitors, beginning with those who have come from the more distant villages ; and when all have got their share they prepare to go home. Only the lower jaw and the lungs are not given away ; they remain the property of the owner of the pig ; and a specially large jaw-bone with big tusks will be treasured for many years as a trophy of the feast.

Some of the pigs from the jungle are let out, one by one in the latter part of the afternoon. These are the savage ones ; and someone who is skilled in catching and holding pigs by the ears is chosen to play with them. If, as sometimes happens, a man is accidentally bitten or ripped by the boar's tusk, in the arm or leg, the boar is at once speared by those standing by. It were an abomination (" sin ") for young folks to eat the flesh of a boar which has gashed a man ; only old folks may eat this.

Some of the guests may have gone home after getting their share of the pork ; but most stay on until after the playing with the pigs. Nearly all however depart that evening or night.

On the following day the fat pigs are killed and reduced to lard, which is stored in cocoanut shells ; and all through next night dancing is kept up, a number of people from the neighbouring villages joining them again.

On the next morning they make preparation for digging up the dead. They cut down cocoanut leaves, and partition off the " good " (*i.e.*, ceremonially clean) houses in " el-panam " (*i.e.* the cemetery quarter where are the birth and death houses, and also the public hall, and other " good " houses, and also the traders shops). This fence of upright leaves runs completely round the cemetery, except on the side of the place where the bones are thrown away by those who are ceremonially unclean ; for they go out that way. Sometimes they are engaged in digging up the dead for one or two whole days, if there have been many deaths.

Then the bones are dug up ; and each person's bones are placed separately on the spathe of a variety of lofty palm, and bound round with new cloth, just as the fresh corpse had been bound round, only the bones of persons who have been a good while dead, say two years or so, are dug up ; for otherwise there would be flesh still on them, though the graves are always in ground of coral formation. All the bones are thus wrapped up, and placed in the " unclean " houses, where they will remain all night, and where also those " unclean " through contact with the graves and bones will sleep.

On the morrow the palm spathe and the cloth is torn off, and " what is to be thrown away " (*i.e.*, most of the bones) is thrown away ; whilst the bones of some rich or revered person will be buried again, and sometimes yet again at the next Ossuary Feast. In Nankuri the skull is put on a plate, and food is served to it, whilst the people are having their own food around ; but this is not done in Car Nicobar.

Before digging up the bones they will draw what water may be required for use until the end of the function, and this they will cover over that it may not be polluted by the breeze which may pass over the bones.

There will be a dance all through the night after the digging up of the bones, and also after the filling in of the graves the next day. People of the neighbouring villages are invited to come to these dances ; and the " unclean " (men and women) form a group of dancers by themselves ; for other people may not touch them with their hands. The fence of cocoanut leaves is left standing for some time ; and perhaps for a month or two the unclean may not touch (with their fingers) even their own food or their cigarettes.

An unfixed number of days after the digging up of the bones, they have a special dance all night. On the following morning they have a crude sort of single-stick fencing with a very brittle kind of wood. If a piece of wood snaps off the end of the stick of the assailant, and strikes the other on the back, that one is supposed to be beaten. Then follow wrestling matches ; and after that the leaves forming the fence round the cemetery are thrown aside, and the cloth and spoon decorations of the houses are stowed away.

Again after a short time, two or three of the people will go to some other village to challenge them to a big boat race. If those who have been sent do not return immediately, they know that the challenge has been accepted.

Again after the big boat race they have a big ma-a-fāi dance, which they invite the people from other villages to perform, the hosts not taking part in it. This brings the Ossuary Feast to a close.

Note.—The ma-a-fāi are the novices for the witch-doctorate ; and the ma-a-fāi dances, in which lay-folks (male and female) take part are no doubt in their origin religious, but in character do not differ widely from the other dances.

The above account is for the most part translated from composition exercises, written in Nicobarese by children in the Car Nicobar Mission School.

G. W.

APPENDIX N.

Nicobarese Folk-lore.

NOTE BY THE REV. G. WHITEHEAD.

The Car Nicobarese have a rich folk-lore, and much of this is very familiarly known even to the young children. Much of this folk-lore is widely different from anything published ; but in the opinion of Sir R. C. Temple would probably be found to be allied to the folk-lore of the Oceanic islanders, even as far afield as Madagascar. A number of these stories are about to be published in the *Indian Antiquary*. As a specimen, the Car Nicobarese variant of the story of the deluge may be given.

" Once upon a time there was a great flood in this land, and the whole surface of it was covered with water. One man, however, was fortunate enough to swim to a great tree which was not entirely immersed in the water. He climbed the tree and lived up in the branches of it until the waters were assuaged. Whenever he saw any cocoanuts come floating his way in the water, or any pigs and fowls (with distended stomachs), he would swim out to them and bring them in ; and eat them up in the branches of the tree.

At last the rain stopped, and then little by little the waters decreased, and he got a little more room ; and at last was able to get down to the solid earth.

Then when the waters were assuaged, he spied a bitch hitched up among the branches of a tree, its ear being spiked by the great thorn of the *kun-hiol* (*i.e.*, the thorny palm). He went to it and released it, and took it with him, and made it his wife ; and they lived together, the bitch and the man ; and they had offspring which was human.

So the people of these parts in the wearing of the *kisāt* (*i.e.*, their very scanty loin cloth) copy the dog, for it has tails like a dog's tail ; and also the band they wear round their head, has ears pricked up like a dog's ears. They say too that they are the children (descendants) of that dog (bitch)".

G. W.

APPENDIX O.

Folk-lore stories obtained from Mr. E. Hart, Car Nicobar.

I. The history of the girl in the moon.

There was once a woman who had four children ; one of them was a baby whose name was Tö-mi-röök. The names of the others were, " Industrious ", " One who minds her own business ", and " Story-teller ". They were all girls.

One day the mother sent the three girls to weed the garden while she stayed at home to mind the baby.

Soon the sun got hot, and Story-teller swung on the branches of a tree and would not work. The others got very sunburnt and asked Story-teller to come and help ; but she only laughed, and later on she slipped away and went home. She put dust on her head and told her mother that she had done all the work, and that the other two had played, and were now idling on the way home.

The mother told Story-teller to get her dinner, and threatened to punish the other two. When they came in she thrust some food at them, but said nothing, and the two girls were very sad, but they ate their food quietly.

When they had eaten the mother asked " Did you like your dinner ? " " Yes " they said, " it was all right ". " Ho Ho " she laughed, " well it was mixed with filth from the baby. I did it because you were so idle and disobedient ". The two children were very sad, and set out to run away.

They knew they would be found if they remained in the island, so they decided to go up to the moon. They tried to go up by way of a creeper, but it broke, so they began to climb up a cob-web. One of them remembered a little box that she had left in the house, and ran back to get it, but her mother caught her and would not let her go. The other girl came down to see where her sister was, and the mother caught her by the foot. There was a long tussle, and the poor girl's ankle was sprained, but she got free at last and climbed up to the moon.

The wicked mother tried to follow, but the web broke and let her down.

So the girl lay down in the moon with her box for a pillow, and there she still is as everybody may see when the moon is lit up.

II. The story of the Great Fish.

Two big girls were cleaning tripe on some rocks at low tide. Just there the sea was very deep, and one of them let the knife fall into the sea. It was at once swallowed by a great fish called Ka-hu-kö.

" Oh, quick, dive down and get the knife ", cried the other girl ; so she dived down, and was at once swallowed by the fish. The other girl waited for a long time playing with a pebble, and at last she too dived down into the deep water to look for the knife, only to meet the same fate as the other girl.

The big fish swam away into the ocean with the girls in his belly.

After a time the girls began to get hungry, and the fish said. " Why don't you cut and eat some of my liver ?" They took him at his word and ate a lot of his liver. This happened several times, and the fish was uncomfortable about it, so he spat out the girls on a rock in the midst of the ocean, and swam away.

After a time a shark came and said " Don't be afraid, I am looking for you, get on my back and I'll carry you back home."

So the shark carried them back to the rock they had dived from, and they went home.

III. A domestic tragedy.

A man and his wife had three children, and lived in the jungle. One day the man went to catch fish, and bade the children collect cocoanut shells to make a fire.

The woman took a sharp knife and whetted it while the children made the fire. When the fire was ready she called the eldest boy to her and said, " Come, I will shave your head ". So he came and sat down before her, when, horror !—gash !! she cut off his head !!.

She called the second child and did the same, and threw both their heads into the fire.

Then she called the youngest child, but he would not come. He said, " No, no, you will cut my head off as you have done to the others ". But she said, " No, no, I will never serve you so for you are my favourite, you are the one who half chews my betel nut for me ". So at last he came, and she cut off his head too.

When the father returned he naturally asked where the children were. "I don't know", said the mother, "in the jungle I suppose". So he called them, but of course nobody answered. Again he asked his wife where they were, but she only told him lies. "Never mind", she said, "come and eat your dinner." So he ate his dinner, and she sat by him; when he had finished his wife said. "Well, do you know you have eaten your own children's flesh?" Then a change came over her, and she became a sea eagle, and as she flew away she cried "Ank, ank, ank".

As for the man he leaned back and beat his head against a post and cried. So he became an owl, and goes about always crying and bewailing his grief.

IV. The discovery of Chaura.

Long long ago the people of Car Nicobar did not know that there was any other country besides this island. They called it "pa-nam", that is to say, the world. True there were wild tales of enormous canoes; some said they were birds with white wings, seen far away across the sea; but most folks thought it was all a dream.

At last some folks made a toy canoe from the dry spathe of the cocoanut flower. The people set up leaves for sails, and put in a cargo of little yams; then they set it adrift in the sea, and away it went merrily over the water.

After some months the little canoe came back, and in it were some very tiny cooking pots. Now the people of Car Nicobar had never seen a cooking pot, so they did not know what to make of these pretty little things, till somebody put some water into one, and as it did not leak he set it on the fire and boiled some water in it; then they put down some bits of yam in and they were boiled too and found to be very good.

Then the people said. "Perhaps there are big pots in the place where the little ones come from", so they again sent off the little canoe, and followed it across the sea in their big canoes. Far far it went for a whole night and day, and at last the men saw an island over the sea, so they paddled to it. They were almost missing it, but some canoes came out to meet them, and so they came to Chaura.

There they saw big canoes to carry more than twenty men, and also big pots, so they bought some pots and brought them home with great pride and joy.

From that time there has been trade between the two islands, and the people have been great friends.

V. Bats.

Long ago before there were any bats on Car Nicobar a ship from a foreign country was wrecked at Arong, on the west coast. The stormy wind drove her on the rocks, for there is only a very narrow landing place at Arong, not big enough for a ship, so the vessel was broken to pieces.

Only a few of the sailors got to land, and these did not know the way, so they struck in land and came to the land of the devils. Their clothes were all torn and dirty, and they climbed the trees to get food. Then the devils turned them into bats; the big folk into big bats; the middle sized folks into middle sized bats; and the boys into little bats: and that is how the bats first came to Car Nicobar, for before that time none had ever been seen.

VI. The origin of the cocoanut.

There was once a man who worked magic, and made water flow out of his elbow. Such a man is dangerous, being possessed of a devil, so the people chopped his head off, and threw it into the jungle. After a time a tree grew out of the skull, and at last fruits as big as a man's head grew on it, and these fruits were full of water. Now water is very scarce on the island; but nobody would drink the water of the cocoanut tree until, one day, a sick man almost at the point of death was so parched with thirst that he was given some cocoanut water to drink, and from that time he began to recover. So all sick people were given cocoanut water to drink and in time everybody drank it.

VII. The story of the magic man.

Once upon a time there was a man named Öt-nya-hum-ku. He could read peoples thoughts, and when he went out in the rain he did not get wet.

One day he went out to get bread-fruit for dinner, whilst his wife collected sticks and drew the water.

As he did not come back she went to see what was the matter, and found him up a tree chopping at the fruit; but as soon as he cut through a stem it joined together again as if he had cut through water, and so he could not gather any fruits.

Then his wife went up the tree and cut the bread-fruit, and they took them home; and the wife thought very much about this matter.

Another time the men were hunting pigs, and the only man who had a chopper was Öt-nya-hum ku; but no sooner did he cut a path through the bushes than the branches grew together again, and so the others could not follow the dogs and pigs. They got disgusted at this, and went home leaving all the spoils of the chase to him.

After a long time he died, and they put his body up in a tree; but in a short time he came to life again, and his wife and all his friends wondered very much.

Years passed by, and at last he died again, and as he lay dying he said, "When I am dead leave a hole down into my grave, for in three days I shall rise up again. You must dig me up and I shall live on; but if you do not dig me up I shall die, and live no more." But in three days the smell from the hole into the grave was so bad that they filled it up with sand, and so the magic man never came to life any more.

VIII. The origin of sharks.

Once upon a time there was a tribe of people on the east coast of the island who were very savage. They also knew much magic, and could bewitch people. So the people of those parts rose up and killed many of those savages, and drove the rest to the west side of the island.

These savages would kill a man at sight, and they would come creeping through the jungle to the villages in hope of killing somebody unawares.

Now it happened that a boy was going through the jungle carrying his little brother on his shoulder. He heard a person walking behind him, but took no notice till his brother cried out, "Oh, I am hurt with a thorn;" but it was really the man walking behind who had stuck him in the thigh with a spear.

"Don't tease the child, you'll make him fall" cried the elder boy, who thought somebody was teasing the child by pinching him.

In a moment the savage man drove his spear into the child's body, under the arm, and killed him. The elder lad let his brother fall, and ran to the village to tell his parents what had happened.

Then the villagers rose up in their wrath and attacked those savages. Many were killed, and some were driven down to the sea shore.

When the savages saw that they were doomed to be slain they turned themselves into sharks by magic; and now, all along the coast there are man-eating sharks who are the terror of the fishermen.

IX. The man who came back.

There was once a man who went with other men, each in his own canoe, to barter with the men on a ship for bread and tobacco in exchange for cocoanuts and fruit. He did not notice that the ship was moving, and so got carried away to a foreign land where he married and had two children. He used to go in a boat and catch fish, and so he became very well-to-do.

One day he saw a boat near the shore, so he got some food and water and went off in it, leaving his wife and children behind.

He rowed, and then set his sail, and after many days he got back to his own land.

He found the people were keeping a feast in his memory; for he was given up for dead; and everyone was dancing and singing, for it was dark.

He went to the pens where the pigs are kept and felt their ears. "Why these are my own pigs", he thought. Then he climbed a tree to get a cocoanut to drink, and some people who heard the noise called out, "Hi! that tree is tabu for the dead man". "What dead man?", he asked. When they gave the name he said "why that's me, I'm not dead". When he came down they saw who it was, and he went to the house, and told his story amid great rejoicings.

APPENDIX P.

The following note on the recurring seasonal religious ceremonies observed by the Car Nicobarese was obtained from John Richardson, a native of Car Nicobar.

Richardson was educated in the Car Nicobar Mission School, and afterwards was for some years in a school in Mandalay; first as scholar, and afterwards as teacher; and he is now Catechist and teacher in his old school at Mus in Car Nicobar.

This note is published in the form in which it came into my hands, without alteration, except for the correction of a few clerical errors.

R. F. L.

Religious ceremonies of the Car Nicobarese throughout the year.

January.—Fa-nang-nya el pan-am, (fa-nang-nya is the abstract noun of the verb "fang," to burn. El pan-am is simply the beach where public buildings, grave yard, dead house, and birth houses are).

In the month of December rattan leaves are stuck across the el pan-am to keep off the evil spirits which bring sickness to the people during the N. E. monsoon.

In January these leaves are pulled up and gathered in a heap on the beach, where they are burnt.

On that occasion the leaves which are used as medicine are displayed hung in the houses at el pan-am, in honour of the events.

February.—In this month the spirits of the dwelling houses are honoured. Fishes are caught from the sweet water ponds in the interior. Small fishes are stuck on sticks, and placed over the entrances of the houses. ("Ke-la kapa-ti," *i.e.*, to put up fish for the houses.)

March.—"Ke-la ok pa-ti", the putting up of the young cocoanuts in the houses.

On this occasion the spirits of the sea fishes are honoured. In the night men go out in several canoes to catch the curve fishes. The fishes are attracted by the light of the torches, and when they come alongside the canoes they are speared. In the morning everyone brings his catch to el pan-am on the beach with several young cocoanuts and tender leaves of cocoanut palm. The fishes are cut up into small bits, and stuck on the young cocoanuts with the leaves. In each hut three of these young cocoanuts are to be hung.

This is the offering to spirits of the deep, in order that they may not get angry, and send sickness through the eating of the fishes.

This is the calmest of the months, and trips to Chaura Island can be taken twice; and people go far out to sea to catch fish by lines and hooks.

April.—In this month fire festival is held.

When the moon is waning the whole night is lighted with cocoanut shells. Dancing goes on the whole night; followed by wrestling in the morning.

After this performance no light should be shown at el pan-am till about the waning of May, when the harvest festival will be held.

May.—In this month "Kun-seu-rö" or the making of pudding is held. Yams, ripe and green plantains are scraped. First of all cocoanuts are scraped, and oil is extracted. When the oil is refined the scraped yams, and ripe and green plantains are put in the Chaura pots. The pudding has to be stirred the whole night till it is quite cooked, in order that it may not stick on the side of the pot. This has to be done at el pan-am under the houses.

The next morning each family has to kill a pig. The village is decorated with tender cocoanut leaves, which are wound round the top of a stick, and over them some young cocoanuts are cut crosswise and put on the stick; then pig's blood is sprinkled on the cocoanut leaves, and pudding on the young cocoanuts.

All the best produces of the land are hung among the decorations in the houses, such as the largest size of yams, cocoanuts, pineapples, jackfruits, as well as some of the puddings.

The men who hang up the decorations in the house will shout out, "may this season be a prosperous one; plenty of pigs, cocoanuts, yams, etc., and may a pretty girl be willing to wed with me", and so on.

The next day is a day of rest. In the evening the boys will go to el pan-am where they start the game of spearing the young cocoanuts which were stuck on the decorations. They are collected in one place, and the boys stand in a long line; a man throws each young cocoanut in front of the boys, and as the nut rolls on the ground the boys try to hit it. When they have done that at el pan-am they will go into the village to perform the same thing.

Next day is a hunting day for the wild pig.

June.—No ceremony in this month.

July.—The bad spirits are driven away, and put on a raft. The spirits of the dead have rendered help, and so they are honoured. Each relation of the dead has to provide anything that is demanded of them; kill chickens and pigs. These are handed to the Ta-mi-lua-na, or the Seers, who are the only persons that can approach them. They were Ma-a-fai before they become Ta-mi-lua-na.

August.—The first festival of fishing with line and hook after the rough weather. The usual offerings are put in the house; three young cocoanuts are hung with bits of fish, and ferns are placed on the wall of the house all round, with bits of fish each.

September.—Second festival of fishing with line and hooks. This time they go to the west coast for the first time. (Offering as in August.)

October.—The putting on of the Banyan leaves at the el pan-am to change the direction of the wind from S. W. to N. E.

November.—Driving of the bad spirits as in July; but are not sent away on a raft as the wind is contrary. They are simply killed by the Ta-mi-lua-nas, and thrown into the sea.

The spirits of the dead are not fed either.

December.—The putting up the rattan leaves on the beach to keep off the bad spirits which bring sickness generally at this time of year.

APPENDIX Q.

Note by John Richardson on "tabus" and ceremonies in connection with the annual trip to Chaura for the purchase of the earthenware cooking pots made there.

Several things are tabu'd or forbidden when a canoe is newly bought from Chaura, *e.g.*, bats ought not to be eaten, — reason, their wings might blind the eyes, and people will not be able to find their way to Chaura. Octopus fish should not be eaten as it is bad for those travelling on the sea, as it is known to have attacked ships. Splitting of wood is forbidden to prevent the canoe from splitting of itself; and many other things. These are observed for months, even for a whole year before the canoe takes its first trip to Chaura and back.

When a boy is taken to Chaura for the first time the blood of a chicken is sprinkled all over his body before the starting from Car Nicobar, and after the arrival at Chaura.

After coming back from Chaura there will be a canoe race, and then strips of pork are tied up and hung over the body of the boy for about one or two hours. After that raw eggs are crushed on his head. This continues for one or two days. Silver wire is wound round both his arms and legs, like a ma-a-fai. Seeds of pandanus are stringed and hung on him. The boy keeps a stick to keep off the other boys from getting the seeds. Several boys would hang about him trying to snatch the seeds without being caught.

PART II.

Imperial Tables.

NOTES.—(1) Tables IV and V are blank for the Andamans and Nicobars as there is no urban population in these Islands.

(2) Tables IXXIV, XVIII, XIX, XXI and XXII of the series of Imperial Census Tables have not been prepared.

TABLE I.—AREA, HOUSES AND POPULATION.

LOCALITY.	Area in Square miles.	Towns.	Villages.	OCCUPIED HOUSES. Total.	In Towns.	In Villages.	POPULATION. Persons. Total.	Persons. Urban.	Persons. Rural.	Males. Total.	Males. Urban.	Males. Rural.	Females. Total.	Females. Urban.	Females. Rural.
1	2	3	4	5	6	7	8	9	10	11	12	13	14	15	16
ANDAMANS AND NICOBARS.	**3,143**	..	**212**	**3,310**	..	**3,310**	**27,086**	..	**27,086**	**20,793**	..	**20,793**	**6,293**	..	**6,293**
Andamans	**635**	..	**132**	**1,734**	..	**1,734**	**17,814**	..	**17,814**	**15,551**	..	**15,551**	**2,263**	..	**2,263**
Port Blair		..	65	1,562	..	1,562	15,675	..	15,675	13,747	..	13,747	1,928	..	1,928
Rest of Andamans	635	..	67	172	..	172	2,139	..	2,139	1,804	..	1,804	335	..	335
Enumerated		..	7	172	..	172	1,562	..	1,562	1,494	..	1,494	68	..	68
Estimated		..	*60	..	..	..	577	..	577	310	..	310	267	..	267
Nicobars	**2,508**	..	**80**	**1,576**	..	**1,576**	**9,272**	..	**9,272**	**5,242**	..	**5,242**	**4,030**	..	**4,030**
Enumerated	2,508	..	63	1,576	..	1,576	8,897	..	8,897	5,052	..	5,052	3,845	..	3,845
Estimated		..	*17	..	..	..	375	..	375	190	..	190	185	..	185

* As the number of villages of the estimated populations could not be ascertained the number given in the 1911 Table has been shown.

TABLE II.—VARIATION IN POPULATION SINCE 1881.

LOCALITY.	Persons. 1921	1911.	1901.	1891.	1881.	Variation, Increase (+), Decrease (—). 1911 to 1921.	1901 to 1911.	1891 to 1901.	1881 to 1891.	Net variation in period 1881-1921. Increase (+) Decrease, (—).	Males. 1921.	1911.	1901.	1891.	1881.	Females. 1921.	1911.	1901.	1891.	1881.
1	2	3	4	5	6	7	8	9	10	11	12	13	14	15	16	17	18	19	20	21
ANDAMANS AND NICOBARS	**27,086**	**26,459**	**24,649**	**15,609**	**14,628**	+627	+1,810	+9,040	+981	+12,458	**20,793**	**19,570**	**18,695**	**13,375**	**12,640**	**6,293**	**6,889**	**5,854**	**2,234**	**1,988**
Andamans	**17,814**	**17,641**	**18,138**	**15,609**	**14,628**	+173	—497	+2,529	+981	+3,186	**15,551**	**14,737**	**15,158**	**13,375**	**12,640**	**2,263**	**2,904**	**2,980**	**2,234**	**1,988**
Port Blair	15,675	16,324	16,256	15,609	14,628	—649	+68	+647	+981	+1,047	13,747	14,109	14,122	13,375	12,640	1,928	2,215	2,134	2,234	1,988
Rest of Andamans	2,139	1,317	1,882	..	..	+822	—565	..	..	..	1,804	628	1,036	..	..	335	689	846	..	..
Enumerated	1,562	1,317*	1,882*	..	..	+822	—565	..	..	..	1,494	628*	1,036	..	..	68	689	846	..	..
Estimated	577			..	..			..	..	..	310			..	..	267			..	..
Nicobars	**9,272**	**8,818**	**6,511**	..	..	+454	+2,307	..	..	..	**5,242**	**4,833**	**3,537**	..	..	**4,030**	**3,985**	**2,974**	..	..
Enumerated	8,897	8,443	6,511*	..	..	+454	+2,307	..	..	..	5,052	4,643	3,537*	..	..	3,845	3,800	2,974	..	..
Estimated	375	375		..	..	..		..	..	..	190	190		..	..	185	185		..	..

* Estimated.

TABLE III.—Towns and Villages classified by Population.

Locality.	Total number of inhabited Towns and Villages.	Population.	Under 500.		500—1,000.		1,000—2,000.	
			Number.	Population.	Number.	Population.	Number.	Population.
1	2	3	4	5	6	7	8	9
ANDAMANS AND NICOBARS.	**212**	**27,086**	**195**	**14,258**	**13**	**8,077**	**4**	**4,751**
Andamans	**132**	**17,814**	**120**	**8,416**	**9**	**5,659**	**3**	**3,739**
Port Blair	65	15,675	53	6,277	9	5,659	3	3,739
Rest of Andamans	67	2,139	67	2,139	....	....	....	....
Enumerated	7	1,562	7	1,562	....	....	....	....
Estimated	60	577	60	577	....	....	....	....
Nicobars	**80**	**9,272**	**75**	**5,842**	**4**	**2,418**	**1**	**1,012**
Enumerated	63	8,897	58	5,467	4	2,418	1	1,012
Estimated	17	375	17	375	....	....	....	....

TABLE VI.—Religion.

Note.—In this Table it is assumed that the whole of the estimated population is Animist by religion.

Religion.	Andamans and Nicobars.			Port Blair.			Rest of Andamans.			Nicobars.		
	Persons.	Males.	Females.	Persons.	Males.	Females.	Persons.	Males.	Females.	Persons.	Males.	Females.
1	2	3	4	5	6	7	8	9	10	11	12	13
All Religions	**27,086**	**20,793**	**6,293**	**15,675**	**13,747**	**1,928**	**2,139**	**1,804**	**335**	**9,272**	**5,242**	**4,030**
Hindu	8,880	7,520	1,360	8,665	7,332	1,333	209	182	27	6	6	...
Brahmanic	*8,814*	*7,455*	*1,359*	*8,599*	*7,267*	*1,332*	*209*	*182*	*27*	*6*	*6*	...
Arya	*66*	*65*	*1*	*66*	*65*	*1*	...	...	...	...	...	...
Sikh	390	366	24	387	363	24	...	...	...	3	3	...
Buddhist	2,652	2,580	72	2,405	2,361	44	132	118	14	115	101	14
Musalman	4,104	3,650	454	3,840	3,394	446	74	67	7	190	189	1
Christian	1,586	1,461	125	378	297	81	1,147	1,127	20	61	37	24
Animist	9,174	4,917	4,257	...	...	...	577	310	267	8,597	4,607	3,990
Confucian	300	299	1	...	...	...	...	...	...	300	299	1

TABLE VII.—AGE, SEX AND CIVIL CONDITION—PART I.—GENERAL TABLE.

NOTE—The estimated population noted below is excluded from this Table :—

Andamanese 577
Nicobarese 375

AGE.	POPULATION.			UNMARRIED.			MARRIED.			WIDOWED.		
	Persons.	Males.	Females.	Persons.	Males.	Females.	Persons.	Males.	Females.	Persons.	Males.	Females.
1	2	3	4	5	6	7	8	9	10	11	12	13
						All Religions.						
0—1 .	410	237	173	410	237	173	...	...	...	...	...	...
1—2 .	141	78	63	141	78	63	...	...	...	...	...	...
2—3 .	270	140	130	270	140	130	...	...	...	...	...	...
3—4 .	341	179	162	340	178	162	1	1	...	...	...	...
4—5 .	390	221	169	388	221	167	2	...	2	...	...	...
Total 0—5 .	***1,552***	***855***	***697***	***1,549***	***854***	***695***	***3***	***1***	***2***	...	...	...
5—10 .	1,488	819	669	1,474	810	664	10	5	5	4	4	...
10—15 .	1,503	822	681	1,422	808	614	77	14	63	4	...	4
15—20 .	1,420	915	505	1,088	811	277	301	96	205	31	8	23
20—25 .	2,135	1,696	439	868	828	40	1,140	793	347	127	75	52
25—30 .	3,544	2,862	682	914	893	21	2,302	1,748	554	328	221	107
30—35 .	4,318	3,729	589	1,012	993	19	2,903	2,401	502	403	335	68
35—40 .	3,913	3,389	524	690	680	10	2,799	2,359	440	424	350	74
40—45 .	2,617	2,319	298	419	407	12	1,853	1,646	207	345	266	79
45—50 .	1,394	1,182	212	164	160	4	1,058	907	151	172	115	57
50—55 .	885	747	138	95	92	3	627	543	84	163	112	51
55—60 .	377	279	98	26	24	2	272	202	70	79	53	26
60—65 .	517	370	147	26	26	...	294	256	38	197	88	109
65—70 .	202	146	56	9	7	2	97	89	8	96	50	46
70 and over.	269	163	106	13	10	3	97	75	22	159	78	81
TOTAL .	**26,134**	**20,293**	**5,841**	**9,769**	**7,403**	**2,366**	**13,833**	**11,135**	**2,698**	**2,532**	**1,755**	**777**
						Hindu.						
0—1 .	82	44	38	82	44	38	...	...	...	...	...	...
1—2 .	49	28	21	49	28	21	...	...	...	...	...	...
2—3 .	76	34	42	76	34	42	...	...	...	...	...	...
3—4 .	86	40	46	85	39	46	1	1	...	...	...	...
4—5 .	66	32	34	64	32	32	2	...	2	...	...	...
Total 0—5 .	***359***	***178***	***181***	***356***	***177***	***179***	***3***	***1***	***2***	...	...	...
5—10 .	346	187	159	343	187	156	3	...	3	...	...	...
10—15 .	239	105	134	203	105	98	34	...	34	2	...	2
15—20 .	228	123	105	101	92	9	119	29	90	8	2	6
20—25 .	647	539	108	231	229	2	372	282	90	44	28	16
25—30 .	1,267	1,104	163	340	334	6	789	661	128	138	109	29
30—35 .	1,805	1,653	152	444	439	5	1,174	1,047	127	187	167	20
35—40 .	1,473	1,380	93	288	288	...	1,020	946	74	165	146	19
40—45 .	1,116	1,031	85	182	182	...	800	734	66	134	115	19
45—50 .	514	481	33	84	83	1	381	358	23	49	40	9
50—55 .	372	335	37	40	40	...	274	249	25	58	46	12
55—60 .	139	122	17	17	16	1	94	88	6	28	18	10
60—65 .	150	115	35	13	13	...	76	69	7	61	33	28
65—70 .	59	43	16	2	2	...	24	23	1	33	18	15
70 and over	100	59	41	6	6	...	36	32	4	58	21	37
TOTAL .	**8,814**	**7,455**	**1,359**	**2,650**	**2,193**	**457**	**5,199**	**4,519**	680	**965**	**743**	**222**
						Arya.						
0—1 .	...	...	...	...	...	...	...	...	...	...	...	...
1—2 .	...	...	...	...	...	...	...	...	...	...	...	...
2—3 .	...	...	...	...	...	...	...	...	...	...	...	...
3—4 .	...	...	...	...	...	...	...	...	...	...	...	...
4—5 .	...	...	...	...	...	...	...	...	...	...	...	...
Total 0—5 .	...	...	...	...	...	...	...	...	...	...	...	...
5—10 .	...	...	...	...	...	...	...	...	...	...	...	...
10—15 .	1	1	...	1	1	...	...	...	...	...	...	...
15—20 .	8	8	...	7	7	...	...	...	...	1	1	...
20—25 .	9	9	...	3	3	...	6	6	...	...	...	...
25—30 .	10	10	...	2	2	...	8	8	...	...	...	...
30—35 .	10	10	...	2	2	...	7	7	...	1	1	...
35—40 .	10	9	1	2	2	...	8	7	1	...	...	...
40—45 .	11	11	...	4	4	...	4	4	...	3	3	...
45—50 .	5	5	...	...	...	...	3	3	...	2	2	...
50—55 .	...	...	...	...	...	...	...	...	...	...	...	...
55—60 .	...	...	...	...	...	...	...	...	...	...	...	...
60—65 .	1	1	...	...	...	...	1	1	...	...	...	...
65—70 .	1	1	...	...	...	...	1	1	...	...	...	...
70 and over	...	...	...	...	...	...	...	...	...	...	...	...
TOTAL .	**66**	**65**	**1**	**21**	**21**	...	**38**	**37**	**1**	**7**	**7**	...

Age.	Population.			Unmarried.			Married.			Widowed.		
	Persons.	Males.	Females.	Persons.	Males.	Females.	Persons.	Males.	Females.	Persons.	Males.	Females.
1	2	3	4	5	6	7	8	9	10	11	12	13
Sikh.												
0—1	1	1	...	1	1	...	...	...	...	...	...	...
1—2	...	...	...	...	...	...	...	...	...	...	...	...
2—3	1	1	...	1	1	...	...	...	...	...	...	...
3—4	...	...	...	...	...	...	...	...	...	...	...	...
4—5	1	1	...	1	1	...	...	...	...	...	...	...
Total 0—5	***3***	***3***	...	***3***	***3***	...	...	...	...	...	...	...
5—10	3	1	2	3	1	2	...	...	...	...	...	...
10—15	4	1	3	1	...	1	3	1	2	...	...	...
15—20	8	8	...	6	6	...	2	2	...	...	...	...
20—25	66	62	4	42	42	...	22	19	3	2	1	1
25—30	64	59	5	36	36	...	21	17	4	7	6	1
30—35	83	75	8	32	32	...	43	36	7	8	7	1
35—40	63	62	1	20	20	...	36	35	1	7	7	...
40—45	47	46	1	15	15	...	24	23	1	8	8	...
45—50	13	13	...	2	2	...	7	7	...	4	4	...
50—55	19	19	...	1	1	...	12	12	...	6	6	...
55—60	2	2	...	...	...	...	1	1	...	1	1	...
60—65	5	5	...	2	2	...	2	2	...	1	1	...
65—70	2	2	...	...	...	...	1	1	...	1	1	...
70 and over	8	8	...	...	...	...	1	1	...	7	7	...
TOTAL	390	**366**	**24**	**163**	**160**	**3**	**175**	**157**	**18**	**52**	**49**	**3**
Buddhist.												
0—1	2	...	2	2	...	2	...	...	...	...	...	...
1—2	1	1	...	1	1	...	...	...	...	...	...	...
2—3	1	...	1	1	...	1	...	...	...	...	...	...
3—4	1	...	1	1	...	1	...	...	...	...	...	...
4—5	2	1	1	2	1	1	...	...	...	...	...	...
Total 0—5	***7***	***2***	***5***	***7***	***2***	***5***	...	...	...	...	...	...
5—10	21	18	3	13	10	3	5	5	...	3	3	...
10—15	13	5	8	11	4	7	2	1	1	...	...	...
15—20	41	34	7	28	25	3	12	8	4	1	1	...
20—25	208	199	9	117	114	3	79	75	4	12	10	2
25—30	438	428	10	188	188	...	230	222	8	20	18	2
30—35	645	637	8	211	210	1	391	385	6	43	42	1
35—40	565	560	5	136	136	...	383	379	4	46	45	1
40—45	370	363	7	81	81	...	248	242	6	41	40	1
45—50	168	162	6	32	32	...	118	112	6	18	18	...
50—55	102	100	2	18	18	...	74	72	2	10	10	...
55—60	39	37	2	...	...	...	31	30	1	8	7	1
60—65	19	19	...	2	2	...	14	14	...	3	3	...
65—70	9	9	...	2	2	...	5	5	...	2	2	...
70 and over	7	7	...	...	...	...	5	5	...	2	2	...
TOTAL	**2,652**	**2,580**	**72**	**846**	**824**	**22**	**1,597**	**1,555**	**42**	**209**	**201**	**8**
Musalman.												
0—1	30	19	11	30	19	11	...	...	...	...	...	...
1—2	29	12	17	29	12	17	...	...	...	...	...	...
2—3	34	16	18	34	16	18	...	...	...	...	...	...
3—4	32	19	13	32	19	13	...	...	...	...	...	...
4—5	29	18	11	29	18	11	...	...	...	...	...	...
Total 0—5	***154***	***84***	***70***	***154***	***84***	***70***	...	...	...	...	...	...
5—10	125	73	52	122	72	50	2	...	2	1	1	...
10—15	106	69	37	93	65	28	12	4	8	1	...	1
15—20	110	74	36	66	62	4	41	12	29	3	...	3
20—25	324	267	57	136	134	2	164	117	47	24	16	8
25—30	597	548	49	214	211	3	329	296	33	54	41	13
30—35	819	768	51	254	252	2	492	450	42	73	66	7
35—40	751	717	34	211	211	...	454	426	28	86	80	6
40—45	508	485	23	104	102	2	340	322	18	64	61	3
45—50	259	247	12	39	39	...	189	181	8	31	27	4
50—55	179	169	10	30	30	...	118	114	4	31	25	6
55—60	62	57	5	7	7	...	40	38	2	15	12	3
60—65	69	56	13	8	8	...	35	31	4	26	17	9
65—70	18	18	...	2	2	...	11	11	...	5	5	...
70 and over	23	18	5	2	2	...	8	7	1	13	9	4
TOTAL	**4,104**	**3,650**	**454**	**1,442**	**1,281**	**161**	**2,235**	**2,009**	**226**	**427**	**360**	**67**

PART I.—GENERAL TABLE

AGE.	POPULATION.			UNMARRIED.			MARRIED.			WIDOWED.		
	Persons.	Males.	Females.	Persons.	Males.	Females.	Persons.	Males.	Females.	Persons.	Males.	Females.
1	2	3	4	5	6	7	8	9	10	11	12	13
					Christian.							
0—1	7	3	4	7	3	4	...	...	...	...	...	...
1—2	8	8	...	8	8	...	...	...	...	...	...	...
2—3	9	7	2	9	7	2	...	...	...	...	...	...
3—4	8	3	5	8	3	5	...	...	...	...	...	...
4—5	2	2	...	2	2	...	...	...	...	...	...	...
Total 0—5	***34***	***23***	***11***	***34***	***23***	***11***	...	...	...	...	...	...
5—10	34	20	14	34	20	14	...	...	...	...	...	...
10—15	29	22	7	29	22	7	...	...	...	...	...	...
15—20	129	123	6	102	99	3	27	24	3	...	...	...
20—25	391	379	12	190	187	3	195	187	8	6	5	1
25—30	351	327	24	60	59	1	281	263	18	10	5	5
30—35	235	214	21	39	38	1	181	164	17	15	12	3
35—40	175	166	9	9	8	1	154	147	7	12	11	1
40—45	120	104	16	16	13	3	91	84	7	13	7	6
45—50	48	46	2	2	2	...	43	41	2	3	3	...
50—55	20	18	2	1	1	...	15	14	1	4	3	1
55—60	9	8	1	...	...	...	6	6	...	3	2	1
60—65	6	6	...	1	1	...	4	4	...	1	1	...
65—70	2	2	...	1	1	...	1	1	...	...	...	...
70 and over	3	3	...	...	...	...	3	3	...	...	...	...
TOTAL	**1,586**	**1,461**	**125**	**518**	**474**	**44**	**1,001**	**938**	**63**	**67**	**49**	**18**
					Animist.							
0—1	288	170	118	288	170	118	...	...	...	...	...	...
1—2	54	29	25	54	29	25	...	...	...	...	...	...
2—3	149	82	67	149	82	67	...	...	...	...	...	...
3—4	214	117	97	214	117	97	...	...	...	...	...	...
4—5	290	167	123	290	167	123	...	...	...	...	...	...
Total 0—5	***995***	***565***	***430***	***995***	***565***	***430***	...	...	...	...	...	...
5—10	959	520	439	959	520	439	...	...	...	...	...	...
10—15	1,102	610	492	1,075	602	473	26	8	18	1	...	1
15—20	884	533	351	771	513	258	95	16	79	18	4	14
20—25	456	207	249	141	111	30	276	81	195	39	15	24
25—30	755	324	431	60	49	11	596	233	363	99	42	57
30—35	640	291	349	18	8	10	548	245	303	74	38	36
35—40	824	443	381	16	7	9	708	383	325	100	53	47
40—45	412	247	165	15	8	7	316	208	108	81	31	50
45—50	376	217	159	4	1	3	307	195	112	65	21	44
50—55	188	101	87	5	2	3	130	78	52	53	21	32
55—60	125	52	73	2	1	1	99	38	61	24	13	11
60—65	267	168	99	...	...	...	162	135	27	105	33	72
65—70	111	71	40	2	...	2	54	47	7	55	24	31
70 and over	128	68	60	5	2	3	44	27	17	79	39	40
TOTAL	**8,222**	**4,417**	**3,805**	**4,068**	**2,389**	**1,679**	**3,361**	**1,694**	**1,667**	**793**	**334**	**459**
					Confucian.							
0—1	...	...	...	...	...	...	...	...	...	...	...	...
1—2	...	...	...	...	...	...	...	...	...	...	...	...
2—3	...	...	...	...	...	...	...	...	...	...	...	...
3—4	...	...	...	...	...	...	...	...	...	...	...	...
4—5	...	...	...	...	...	...	...	...	...	...	...	...
Total 0—5	...	...	...	...	...	...	...	...	...	...	...	...
5—10	...	...	...	...	...	...	...	...	...	...	...	...
10—15	9	9	...	9	9	...	...	...	...	...	...	...
15—20	12	12	...	7	7	...	5	5	...	...	...	...
20—25	34	34	...	8	8	...	26	26	...	...	...	...
25—30	62	62	...	14	14	...	48	48	...	...	...	...
30—35	81	81	...	12	12	...	67	67	...	2	2	...
35—40	52	52	...	8	8	...	36	36	...	8	8	...
40—45	33	32	1	2	2	...	30	29	1	1	1	...
45—50	11	11	...	1	1	...	10	10	...	...	...	...
50—55	5	5	...	...	...	...	4	4	...	1	1	...
55—60	1	1	...	...	...	...	1	1	...	...	...	...
60—65	...	...	...	...	...	...	...	...	...	...	...	...
65—70	...	...	...	...	...	...	...	...	...	...	...	...
70 and over	...	...	...	...	...	...	...	...	...	...	...	...
TOTAL	**300**	**299**	**1**	**61**	**61**	...	**227**	**226**	**1**	**12**	**12**	...

TABLE VII.—Age, sex and Civil Condition. Part II.—Details by Locality.

PORT BLAIR.

Age and Religion.	Population.			Unmarried.		Married.		Widowed.	
	Persons.	Males.	Females.	Males.	Females.	Males.	Females.	Males.	Females.
1	2	3	4	5	6	7	8	9	10
ALL RELIGIONS	**15,675**	**13,747**	**1,928**	**4,422**	**652**	**7,974**	**965**	**1,351**	**311**
0—5	533	274	259	273	257	1	2	...	...
5—10	478	264	214	263	209	...	5	1	...
10—15	352	172	180	167	132	5	45	...	3
15—20	326	177	149	131	19	42	121	4	9
20—40	9,673	8,904	769	2,892	28	5,220	605	792	136
40—60	3,850	3,603	247	657	7	2,509	170	437	70
60 and over	463	353	110	39	...	197	17	117	93
HINDU	**8,599**	**7,267**	**1,332**	**2,143**	**447**	**4,394**	**663**	**730**	**222**
0—5	355	174	181	173	179	1	2	...	...
5—10	333	182	151	182	148	...	3	...	...
10—15	235	103	132	103	96	...	34	...	2
15—20	205	101	104	74	9	25	89	2	6
20—40	5,056	4,556	500	1,271	13	2,842	403	443	84
40—60	2,107	1,935	172	319	2	1,403	120	213	50
60 and over	308	216	92	21	...	123	12	72	80
ARYA	**66**	**65**	**1**	**21**	..	**37**	**1**	**7**	..
0—5	...	...	...	...	...	...	...	...	...
5—10	...	...	...	...	...	...	...	...	...
10—15	1	1	...	1	...	...	...	...	...
15—20	8	8	...	7	...	...	...	1	...
20—40	39	38	1	9	...	28	1	1	...
40—60	16	16	...	4	...	7	...	5	...
60 and over	2	2	...	...	...	2	...	...	...
SIKH	**387**	**363**	**24**	**160**	**3**	**154**	**18**	**49**	**3**
0—5	3	3	...	3	...	...	...	...	...
5—10	3	1	2	1	2	...	...	...	...
10—15	4	1	3	...	1	1	2	...	...
15—20	8	8	...	6	...	2	...	...	...
20—40	274	256	18	130	...	105	15	21	3
40—60	80	79	1	18	...	42	1	19	...
60 and over	15	15	...	2	...	4	...	9	...
BUDDHIST	**2,405**	**2,361**	**44**	**764**	**12**	**1,413**	**24**	**184**	**8**
0—5	3	...	3	...	3	...	...	...	...
5—10	1	1	...	1	...	...	...	...	...
10—15	7	3	4	2	3	1	1	...	...
15—20	27	20	7	13	3	6	4	1	...
20—40	1,736	1,717	19	617	3	989	10	111	6
40—60	610	599	11	129	...	403	9	67	2
60 and over	21	21	...	2	...	14	...	5	...
MUSALMAN	**3,840**	**3,394**	**446**	**1,186**	**159**	**1,852**	**221**	**356**	**66**
0—5	151	82	69	82	69	...	...	...	...
5—10	118	66	52	65	50	...	2	1	...
10—15	97	60	37	57	28	3	8	...	1
15—20	66	32	34	27	4	5	27	...	3
20—40	2,339	2,151	188	769	6	1,181	148	201	34
40—60	962	914	48	174	2	616	31	124	15
60 and over	107	89	18	12	...	47	5	30	13
CHRISTIAN	**378**	**297**	**81**	**148**	**31**	**124**	**38**	**25**	**12**
0—5	21	15	6	15	6	...	...	...	...
5—10	23	14	9	14	9	...	...	...	...
10—15	8	4	4	4	4	...	...	...	...
15—20	12	8	4	4	3	4	1	...	...
20—40	229	186	43	96	6	75	28	15	9
40—60	75	60	15	13	3	38	9	9	3
60 and over	10	10	...	2	...	7	...	1	...

TABLE VII.—Age, Sex and Civil condition. Part II.—Details by Locality.

REST OF ANDAMANS.

AGE AND RELIGION.	Population.			Unmarried.		Married.		Widowed.	
	Persons.	Males.	Females.	Males.	Females.	Males.	Females.	Males.	Females.
1	2	3	4	5	6	7	8	9	10
ALL RELIGIONS	**1,562**	**1,494**	**68**	**408**	**28**	**1,046**	**38**	**40**	**2**
0—5	16	11	5	11	5	...	...	...	...
5—10	21	8	13	8	13	...	...	...	...
10—15	27	18	9	18	9	...	...	...	...
15—20	153	149	4	121	...	28	4	...	...
20—40	1,151	1,115	36	245	1	844	34	26	1
40—60	193	192	1	5	...	173	...	14	1
60 and over	1	1	...	...	...	1	...	...	...
HINDU	**209**	**182**	**27**	**47**	**10**	**123**	**17**	**12**	...
0—5	4	4	...	4	...	...	...	...	...
5—10	13	5	8	5	8	...	...	...	...
10—15	4	2	2	2	2	...	...	...	...
15—20	23	22	1	18	...	4	1	...	...
20—40	131	115	16	16	...	92	16	7	...
40—60	33	33	...	2	...	26	...	5	...
60 and over	1	1	...	...	...	1	...	...	...
BUDDHIST	**132**	**118**	**14**	**35**	**5**	**80**	**9**	**3**	...
0—5	3	2	1	2	1	...	...	...	...
5—10	2	2	...	2	...	...	...	...	...
10—15	6	2	4	2	4	...	...	...	...
15—20	12	12	...	10	...	2	...	...	...
20—40	72	63	9	18	...	45	9	...	...
40—60	37	37	...	1	...	33	...	3	...
60 and over	...	...	...	...	...	...	...	...	...
MUSALMAN	**74**	**67**	**7**	**19**	**2**	**47**	**4**	**1**	**1**
0—5	2	1	1	1	1	...	...	...	...
5—10	1	1	...	1	...	...	...	...	...
10—15	...	...	...	...	...	...	...	...	...
15—20	5	3	2	1	...	2	2	...	...
20—40	56	53	3	16	1	36	2	1	...
40—60	10	9	1	...	...	9	...	...	1
60 and over	...	...	...	...	...	...	...	...	...
CHRISTIAN	**1,147**	**1,127**	**20**	**307**	**11**	**796**	**8**	**24**	**1**
0—5	7	4	3	4	3	...	...	...	...
5—10	5	...	5	...	5	...	...	...	...
10—15	17	14	3	14	3	...	...	...	...
15—20	113	112	1	92	...	20	1	...	...
20—40	892	884	8	195	...	671	7	18	1
40—60	113	113	...	2	...	105	...	6	...
60 and over	...	...	...	...	...	...	...	...	...

TABLE VII.—Age, Sex and Civil Condition. Part II.—Details by Locality.

NICOBARS.

AGE AND RELIGION.	Population.			Unmarried.		Married.		Widowed.	
	Persons.	Males.	Females.	Males.	Females.	Males.	Females.	Males.	Females.
1	2	3	4	5	6	7	8	9	10
ALL RELIGIONS	**8,897**	**5,052**	**3,845**	**2,573**	**1,686**	**2,115**	**1,695**	**364**	**464**
0—5	1,003	570	433	570	433	...	...	...	...
5—10	989	547	442	539	442	5	...	3	...
10—15	1,124	632	492	623	473	9	18	...	1
15—20	941	589	352	559	258	26	80	4	14
20—40	3,086	1,657	1,429	257	61	1,237	1,204	163	164
40—60	1,230	732	498	21	14	616	342	95	142
60 and over	524	325	199	4	5	222	51	99	143
HINDU	**6**	**6**	..	**3**	..	**2**	..	**1**	..
0—5	...	...	...	...	...	...	...	...	...
5—10	...	...	...	...	...	...	...	...	...
10—15	...	...	...	...	...	...	...	...	...
15—20	...	...	...	...	...	...	...	...	...
20—40	5	5	...	3	...	2	...	...	...
40—60	1	1	...	...	...	...	...	1	...
60 and over	...	...	...	...	...	...	...	...	...
SIKH	**3**	**3**	..	..	..	**3**	..	..	..
0—5	...	...	...	...	...	...	...	...	...
5—10	...	...	...	...	...	...	...	...	...
10—15	...	...	...	...	...	...	...	...	...
15—20	...	...	...	...	...	...	...	...	...
20—40	2	2	...	...	...	2	...	...	...
40—60	1	1	...	...	...	1	...	...	...
60 and over	...	...	...	...	...	...	...	...	...
BUDDHIST	**115**	**101**	**14**	**25**	**5**	**62**	**9**	**14**	..
0—5	1	...	1	...	1	...	...	...	...
5—10	18	15	3	7	3	5	...	3	...
10—15	...	...	...	...	...	...	...	...	...
15—20	2	2	...	2	...	...	...	...	...
20—40	48	44	4	13	1	27	3	4	...
40—60	32	26	6	1	...	20	6	5	...
60 and over	14	14	...	2	...	10	...	2	...
MUSALMAN	**190**	**189**	**1**	**76**	..	**110**	**1**	**3**	..
0—5	1	1	...	1	...	...	...	...	...
5—10	6	6	...	6	...	...	...	...	...
10—15	9	9	...	8	...	1	...	...	...
15—20	39	39	...	34	...	5	...	...	...
20—40	96	96	...	23	...	72	...	1	...
40—60	36	35	1	4	...	30	1	1	...
60 and over	3	3	...	...	...	2	...	1	...
CHRISTIAN	**61**	**37**	**24**	**19**	**2**	**18**	**17**	...	**5**
0—5	6	4	2	4	2	...	...	...	...
5—10	6	6	...	6	...	...	...	...	...
10—15	4	4	...	4	...	...	...	...	...
15—20	4	3	1	3	...	...	1	...	...
20—40	31	16	15	1	...	15	15	...	...
40—60	9	3	6	1	...	2	1	...	5
60 and over	1	1	...	...	...	1	...	...	...
ANIMIST	**8,222**	**4,417**	**3,805**	**2,389**	**1,679**	**1,694**	**1,667**	**334**	**459**
0—5	995	565	430	565	430	...	...	...	...
5—10	959	520	439	520	439	...	...	...	...
10—15	1,102	610	492	602	473	8	18	...	1
15—20	884	533	351	513	258	16	79	4	14
20—40	2,675	1,265	1,410	175	60	942	1,186	148	164
40—60	1,101	617	484	12	14	519	333	86	137
60 and over	506	307	199	2	5	209	51	96	143
CONFUCIAN	**300**	**299**	**1**	**61**	..	**226**	**1**	**12**	..
0—5	...	...	...	...	...	...	...	...	...
5—10	...	...	...	...	...	...	...	...	...
10—15	9	9	...	9	...	...	...	...	...
15—20	12	12	...	7	...	5	...	...	...
20—40	229	229	...	42	...	177	...	10	...
40—60	50	49	1	3	...	44	1	2	...
60 and over	...	...	...	...	...	...	...	...	...

TABLE VIII.—Literacy by Religion and Age. Part I.—General Table.

Notes.—1. The estimated population is excluded from this Table.
2. 272 (males 247, females 25) Indian Christians are literate; of whom 165 (males 153, females 12) are literate in English.

Age and Religion.	Population.									Literate in English.		
	Total.			Literate.			Illiterate.					
	Persons.	Males.	Females.	Persons.	Males	Females.	Persons.	Males.	Females.	Persons.	Males.	Females.
1	2	3	4	5	6	7	8	9	10	11	12	13
All Religions	**26,134**	**20,293**	**5,841**	**4,790**	**4,606**	**184**	**21,344**	**15,687**	**5,657**	**670**	**613**	**57**
0—10	3,040	1,674	1,366	34	20	14	3,006	1,654	1,352	11	8	3
10—15	1,503	822	681	90	64	26	1,413	758	655	28	22	6
15—20	1,420	915	505	156	140	16	1,264	775	489	48	44	4
20 and over	20,171	16,882	3,289	4,510	4,382	128	15,661	12,500	3,161	583	539	44
Hindu	**8,814**	**7,455**	**1,359**	**1,713**	**1,657**	**56**	**7,101**	**5,798**	**1,303**	**250**	**243**	**7**
0—10	705	365	340	14	10	4	691	355	336	3	2	1
10—15	239	105	134	37	27	10	202	78	124	12	12	...
15—20	228	123	105	54	50	4	174	73	101	29	28	1
20 and over	7,642	6,862	780	1,608	1,570	38	6,034	5,292	742	206	201	5
Arya	**66**	**65**	**1**	**46**	**46**	..	**20**	**19**	**1**	**10**	**10**	..
0—10	...	...	...	...	...	...	...	...	...	...	...	...
10—15	1	1	...	...	...	...	1	1	...	...	...	...
15—20	8	8	...	2	2	...	6	6	...	1	1	...
20 and over	57	56	1	44	44	...	13	12	1	9	9	...
Sikh	**390**	**366**	**24**	**147**	**142**	**5**	**243**	**224**	**19**	**11**	**11**	..
0—10	6	4	2	...	...	...	6	4	2	...	...	...
10—15	4	1	3	...	...	...	4	1	3	...	...	...
15—20	8	8	...	7	7	...	1	1	...	...	...	...
20 and over	372	353	19	140	135	5	232	218	14	11	11	...
Buddhist	**2,652**	**2,580**	**72**	**1,543**	**1,500**	**43**	**1,109**	**1,080**	**29**	**36**	**34**	**2**
0—10	28	20	8	2	1	1	26	19	7	...	...	...
10—15	13	5	8	9	4	5	4	1	3	...	...	...
15—20	41	34	7	28	22	6	13	12	1	...	...	...
20 and over	2,570	2,521	49	1,504	1,473	31	1,066	1,048	18	36	34	2
Musalman	**4,104**	**3,650**	**454**	**784**	**763**	**21**	**3,320**	**2,887**	**433**	**112**	**108**	**4**
0—10	279	157	122	3	3	...	276	154	122	1	1	...
10—15	106	69	37	32	25	7	74	44	30	10	8	2
15—20	110	74	36	41	39	2	69	35	34	10	10	...
20 and over	3,609	3,350	259	708	696	12	2,901	2,654	247	91	89	2
Christian	**1,586**	**1,461**	**125**	**443**	**386**	**57**	**1,143**	**1,075**	**68**	**250**	**206**	**44**
0—10	68	43	25	15	6	9	53	37	16	7	5	2
10—15	29	22	7	11	7	4	18	15	3	6	2	4
15—20	129	123	6	23	19	4	106	104	2	8	5	3
20 and over	1,360	1,273	87	394	354	40	966	919	47	229	194	35
Animist	**8,222**	**4,417**	**3,805**	**10**	**8**	**2**	**8,212**	**4,409**	**3,803**	..	..	..
0—10	1,954	1,085	869	...	...	...	1,954	1,085	869	...	...	...
10—15	1,102	610	492	...	...	...	1,102	610	492	...	...	...
15—20	884	533	351	...	...	...	884	533	351	...	...	...
20 and over	4,282	2,189	2,093	10	8	2	4,272	2,181	2,091	...	...	...
Confucian	**300**	**299**	**1**	**104**	**104**	..	**196**	**195**	**1**	**1**	**1**	..
0—10	...	...	...	...	...	...	...	...	...	...	...	...
10—15	9	9	...	1	1	...	8	8	...	...	...	...
15—20	12	12	...	1	1	...	11	11	...	...	...	...
20 and over	279	278	1	102	102	...	177	176	1	1	1	...

TABLE VIII.—Literacy by Religion and Age. Part II.—Details by Locality.

PORT BLAIR.

Age and Religion.	Population.									Literate in English.		
	Total.			Literate.			Illiterate.					
	Persons.	Males.	Females.	Persons.	Males.	Females.	Persons.	Males.	Females.	Persons.	Males.	Females.
1	2	3	4	5	6	7	8	9	10	11	12	13
All Religions	**15,675**	**13,747**	**1,928**	**4,105**	**3,942**	**163**	**11,570**	**9,805**	**1,765**	**583**	**529**	**54**
0—10	1,011	538	473	31	17	14	980	521	459	11	8	3
10—15	352	172	180	80	55	25	272	117	155	27	21	6
15—20	326	177	149	99	84	15	227	93	134	45	42	3
20 and over	13,986	12,860	1,126	3,895	3,786	109	10,091	9,074	1,017	500	458	42
Hindu	**8,599**	**7,267**	**1,332**	**1,626**	**1,574**	**52**	**6,973**	**5,693**	**1,280**	**228**	**221**	**7**
0—10	688	356	332	13	9	4	675	347	328	3	2	1
10—15	235	103	132	37	27	10	198	76	122	12	12	...
15—20	205	101	104	42	38	4	163	63	100	29	28	1
20 and over	7,471	6,707	764	1,534	1,500	34	5,937	5,207	730	184	179	5
Arya	**66**	**65**	**1**	**46**	**46**	..	**20**	**19**	**1**	**10**	**10**	..
0—10	...	...	...	...	...	...	...	...	...	...	...	...
10—15	1	1	...	...	...	...	1	1	...	...	...	...
15—20	8	8	...	2	2	...	6	6	...	1	1	...
20 and over	57	56	1	44	44	...	13	12	1	9	9	...
Sikh	**387**	**363**	**24**	**144**	**139**	**5**	**243**	**224**	**19**	**11**	**11**	..
0—10	6	4	2	...	...	...	6	4	2	...	...	...
10—15	4	1	3	...	...	...	4	1	3	...	...	...
15—20	8	8	...	7	7	...	1	1	...	...	...	...
20 and over	369	350	19	137	132	5	232	218	14	11	11	...
Buddhist	**2,405**	**2,361**	**44**	**1,380**	**1,349**	**31**	**1,025**	**1,012**	**13**	**30**	**22**	**1**
0—10	4	1	3	1	...	1	3	1	2	...	...	...
10—15	7	3	4	7	3	4	...	...	...	...	...	...
15—20	27	20	7	19	13	6	8	7	1	...	...	...
20 and over	2,367	2,337	30	1,353	1,333	20	1,014	1,004	10	30	29	1
Musalman	**3,840**	**3,394**	**446**	**643**	**622**	**21**	**3,197**	**2,772**	**425**	**96**	**92**	**4**
0—10	269	148	121	2	2	...	267	146	121	1	1	...
10—15	97	60	37	28	21	7	69	39	30	9	7	2
15—20	66	32	34	18	16	2	48	16	32	9	9	...
20 and over	3,408	3,154	254	595	583	12	2,813	2,571	242	77	75	2
Christian	**378**	**297**	**81**	**266**	**212**	**54**	**112**	**85**	**27**	**208**	**166**	**42**
0—10	44	29	15	15	6	9	29	23	6	7	5	2
10—15	8	4	4	8	4	4	...	...	...	6	2	4
15—20	12	8	4	11	8	3	1	...	1	6	4	2
20 and over	314	256	58	232	194	38	82	62	20	189	155	34

TABLE VIII.—Literacy by Religion and Age. Part II.—Details by Locality.

REST OF ANDAMANS.

Age and Religion.	Population.									Literate in English.		
	Total.			Literate.			Illiterate.					
	Persons.	Males.	Females.	Persons.	Males.	Females.	Persons.	Males.	Females.	Persons.	Males.	Females.
1	2	3	4	5	6	7	8	9	10	11	12	13
All Religions	**1,562**	**1,494**	**68**	**372**	**359**	**13**	**1,190**	**1,135**	**55**	**70**	**68**	**2**
0—10	37	19	18	1	1	...	36	18	18	...	...	...
10—15	27	18	9	5	4	1	22	14	8	...	...	...
15—20	153	149	4	33	32	1	120	117	3	2	1	1
20 and over	1,345	1,308	37	333	322	11	1,012	986	26	68	67	1
Hindu	**209**	**182**	**27**	**82**	**78**	**4**	**127**	**104**	**23**	**21**	**21**	...
0—10	17	9	8	1	1	...	16	8	8	...	...	...
10—15	4	2	2	...	...	...	4	2	2	...	...	...
15—20	23	22	1	12	12	...	11	10	1	...	...	...
20 and over	165	149	16	69	65	4	96	84	12	21	21	...
Buddhist	**132**	**118**	**14**	**95**	**89**	**6**	**37**	**29**	**8**	**3**	**3**	...
0—10	5	4	1	...	...	...	5	4	1	...	...	...
10—15	6	2	4	2	1	1	4	1	3	...	...	...
15—20	12	12	...	7	7	...	5	5	...	...	...	...
20 and over	109	100	9	86	81	5	23	19	4	3	3	...
Musalman	**74**	**67**	**7**	**21**	**21**	...	**53**	**46**	**7**	**6**	**6**	...
0—10	3	2	1	...	...	...	3	2	1	...	...	...
10—15	...	...	...	...	...	...	...	...	...	...	...	...
15—20	5	3	2	2	2	...	3	1	2	...	...	...
20 and over	66	62	4	19	19	...	47	43	4	6	6	...
Christian	**1,147**	**1,127**	**20**	**174**	**171**	**3**	**973**	**956**	**17**	**40**	**38**	**2**
0—10	12	4	8	...	...	...	12	4	8	...	...	...
10—15	17	14	3	3	3	...	14	11	3	...	...	...
15—20	113	112	1	12	11	1	101	101	...	2	1	1
20 and over	1,005	997	8	159	157	2	846	840	6	38	37	1

TABLE VIII.—Literacy by Religion and Age. Part II.—Details by Locality.

NICOBARS.

Age and Religion.	Population. Total. Persons.	Population. Total. Males.	Population. Total. Females.	Population. Literate. Persons.	Population. Literate. Males.	Population. Literate. Females.	Population. Illiterate. Persons.	Population. Illiterate. Males.	Population. Illiterate. Females.	Literate in English. Persons.	Literate in English. Males.	Literate in English. Females.
1	2	3	4	5	6	7	8	9	10	11	12	13
All Religions	**8,897**	**5,052**	**3,845**	**313**	**305**	**8**	**8,584**	**4,747**	**3,837**	**17**	**16**	**1**
0—10	1,992	1,117	875	2	2	...	1,990	1,115	875	...	...	...
10—15	1,124	632	492	5	5	...	1,119	627	492	1	1	...
15—20	941	589	352	24	24	...	917	565	352	1	1	...
20 and over	4,840	2,714	2,126	282	274	8	4,558	2,440	2,118	15	14	1
Hindu	**6**	**6**	..	**5**	**5**	..	**1**	**1**	...	**1**	**1**	...
0—10	...	...	...	...	...	...	...	...	...	...	...	...
10—15	...	...	...	...	...	...	...	...	...	...	...	...
15—20	...	...	...	...	...	...	...	...	...	...	...	...
20 and over	6	6	...	5	5	...	1	1	...	1	1	...
Sikh	**3**	**3**	..	**3**	**3**	..	..	..	..	..	..	...
0—10	...	...	...	...	...	...	...	...	...	...	...	...
10—15	...	...	...	...	...	...	...	...	...	...	...	...
15—20	...	...	...	...	...	...	...	...	...	...	...	...
20 and over	3	3	...	3	3	...	...	...	...	...	...	...
Buddhist	**115**	**101**	**14**	**68**	**62**	**6**	**47**	**39**	**8**	**3**	**2**	**1**
0—10	19	15	4	1	1	...	18	14	4	...	...	...
10—15	...	...	...	...	...	...	...	...	...	...	...	...
15—20	2	2	...	2	2	...	...	...	...	...	...	...
20 and over	94	84	10	65	59	6	29	25	4	3	2	1
Musalman	**190**	**189**	**1**	**120**	**120**	..	**70**	**69**	**1**	**10**	**10**	...
0—10	7	7	...	1	1	...	6	6	...	...	...	...
10—15	9	9	...	4	4	...	5	5	...	1	1	...
15—20	39	39	...	21	21	...	18	18	...	1	1	...
20 and over	135	134	1	94	94	...	41	40	1	8	8	...
Christian	**61**	**37**	**24**	**3**	**3**	..	**58**	**34**	**24**	**2**	**2**	...
0—10	12	10	2	...	...	...	12	10	2	...	...	...
10—15	4	4	...	...	...	...	4	4	...	...	...	...
15—20	4	3	1	...	...	...	4	3	1	...	...	...
20 and over	41	20	21	3	3	...	38	17	21	2	2	...
Animist	**8,222**	**4,417**	**3,805**	**10**	**8**	**2**	**8,212**	**4,409**	**3,803**	...	...	...
0—10	1,954	1,085	869	...	...	...	1,954	1,085	869	...	...	...
10—15	1,102	610	492	...	...	...	1,102	610	492	...	...	...
15—20	884	533	351	...	...	...	884	533	351	...	...	...
20 and over	4,282	2,189	2,093	10	8	2	4,272	2,181	2,091	...	...	...
Confucian	**300**	**299**	**1**	**104**	**104**	...	**196**	**195**	**1**	**1**	**1**	...
0—10	...	...	...	...	...	...	...	...	...	...	...	...
10—15	9	9	...	1	1	...	8	8	...	...	...	...
15—20	12	12	...	1	1	...	11	11	...	...	...	...
20 and over	279	278	1	102	102	...	177	176	1	1	1	...

TABLE X.—LANGUAGE.

NOTE.—The whole population is included in this Table. Though there was no record of language for the estimated Andamanese (577) and Nicobarese ([illegible]75) they have been taken as speaking the tribal languages.

Language.	TOTAL.			ANDAMANS.			NICOBARS		
	Persons.	Males.	Females.	Persons.	Males.	Females.	Persons.	Males.	Females.
1	2	3	4	5	6	7	8	9	10
Total .	**27,086**	**20,793**	**6,293**	**17,814**	**15,551**	**2,263**	**9,272**	**5,242**	**4,030**
A. Vernaculars of India .	*26,502*	*20,265*	*6,237*	*17,549*	*15,340*	*2,209*	*8,953*	*4,925*	*4,028*
Abor	1	1	..	1	1	..	..	..	..
Andamanese . .	577	310		577	310	267	..	..	..
Assamese . . .	18	15	3	18	15	3	..	..	..
Baloch. . . .	48	48	..	48	48		..	..	..
Bengali . . .	1,213	1,161	52	1,212	1,160	52	1	1	..
Bihari	2	2	..	2	2	..	..	..	..
Burmese . . .	2,490	2,428	62	2,409	2,360	49	81	68	13
Gondi	1	1	..	1	1	..	..	..	..
Gujarati . . .	206	199	7	196	189	7	10	10	..
Kanarese . . .	50	50	..	35	35	..	15	15	..
Kandhi. . . .	1	1	..	1	1	..	..	..	..
Karen	10	1	9	5	1	4	5	..	5
Khamti . . .	5	5	..	5	5	..	..	..	..
Kiranti . . .	283	278	5	283	278	5	..	..	..
Malay	107	103	4	106	102	4	1	1	..
Manipuri . . .	2	..	2	2	..	2	..	..	..
Marathi . . .	505	472	33	505	472	33	..	..	..
Moran. . . .	1	1	..	1	1	..	..	..	..
Munda. . . .	251	250	1	251	250	1	..	..	..
Naipali . . .	20	20	..	20	20	..	..	..	..
Nicobarese . . .	8,656	4,647	4,009	..	..	..	8,656	4,647	4,009
Oraon	83	83	..	83	83	..	..	..	..
Oriya	673	646	27	673	646	27	..	..	..
Pahari (unspecified) .	54	43	11	54	43	11	..	..	..
Palaung . . .	2	2	..	2	2	..	..	..	..
Panjabi . . .	1,631	1,513	118	1,630	1,513	117	1	..	1
Pashto. . . .	464	459	5	464	459	5	..	..	..
Rajasthani . . .	7	7	..	7	7	..	..	..	..
Salon	20	20	..	20	20	..		..	..
Sindhi	186	183	3	186	183	3	..	..	..
Tamil	939	802	137	938	801	137	1	1	..
Telegu . . .	385	364	21	385	364	21	..	..	..
Western Hindi . .	7,461	6,003	1,458	7,279	5,821	1,458	182	182	..
Other languages . .	150	147	3	150	147	3	..	..	..
B. Vernaculars of other Asiatic countries.	*364*	*360*	*4*	*45*	*43*	*2*	*319*	*317*	*2*
Arabic . . .	6	6	..	6	6	..	..	..	..
Chinese . . .	336	332	4	17	15	2	319	317	2
Singhalese . . .	22	22	..	22	22	..	..	..	..
C. European Languages .	*220*	*168*	*52*	*220*	*168*	*52*	..	..	..
English. . . .	219	167	52	219	167	52	..	..	..
Portuguese . . .	1	1	..	1	1	..	..	..	..

TABLE XI.—Birth place.

NOTE.—The whole population is included in this Table. Though there was no record of birth place for the estimated populations of the Andamans and Nicobars they have been taken as born in the respective islands.

District, State, Province or Country where born.	Andamans and Nicobars.			District where enumerated.								
				Port Blair.			Rest of Andamans.			Nicobars.		
	Persons.	Males.	Females.	Persons.	Males.	Females.	Persons.	Males.	Females.	Persons.	Males.	Females.
1	2	3	4	5	6	7	8	9	10	11	12	13
Total Population	**27,086**	**20,793**	**6,293**	**15,675**	**13,747**	**1,928**	**2,139**	**1,804**	**335**	**9,272**	**5,242**	**4,030**
A.—Born in India.	***26,362***	***20,090***	***6,272***	***15,320***	***13,410***	***1,910***	***2,095***	***1,760***	***335***	***8,947***	***4,920***	***4,027***
I.—Born in Andamans and Nicobars.	***11,966***	***6,568***	***5,398***	***2,384***	***1,301***	***1,083***	***877***	***574***	***303***	***8,705***	***4,693***	***4,012***
Port Blair	2,581	1,494	1,087	2,331	1,276	1,055	245	214	31	5	4	1
Rest of Andamans	675	375	300	43	15	28	632	360	272	..	..	..
Nicobars	8,710	4,699	4,011	10	10	..	..	..	..	8,700	4,689	4,011
II.—Born in Provinces, Districts or States beyond the Province.	***14,396***	***13,522***	***874***	***12,936***	***12,109***	***827***	***1,218***	***1,186***	***32***	***242***	***227***	***15***
(a) *British Territory*	*13,414*	*12,596*	*818*	*12,037*	*11,266*	*771*	*1,156*	*1,124*	*32*	*221*	*206*	*15*
Ajmer-Merwara	42	39	3	42	39	3	..	..	..	..	..	..
Assam	147	127	20	128	108	20	19	19	..	..	..	..
Baluchistan (*Districts and Administered Territories.*)	67	67	..	67	67	..	..	..	..	..	..	..
Bengal	883	796	87	847	763	84	26	23	3	10	10	..
Bihar and Orissa	1,479	1,406	73	822	756	66	654	647	7	3	..	..
Bombay	1,288	1,245	43	1,056	1,014	42	219	218	1	13	13	..
Burma	2,060	1,994	66	1,751	1,717	34	219	202	17	90	75	15
Central Provinces and Berar.	470	422	48	466	420	46	4	2	2	..	..	..
Coorg	13	13	..	13	13	..	..	..	..	..	..	..
Delhi	35	28	7	32	25	7	1	1	..	2	2	..
Madras including Laccadives.	1,650	1,535	115	1,562	1,447	115	2	2	..	86	86	..
N. W. Frontier Province (*Districts and Administered Territories*).	477	470	7	477	470	7	..	..	..	..	..	..
Punjab	1,688	1,554	134	1,679	1,547	132	4	2	2	5	5	..
United Provinces of Agra and Oudh.	3,115	2,900	215	3,095	2,880	215	8	8	..	12	12	..
(b) *States and Agencies*	*660*	*630*	*30*	*639*	*609*	*30*	..	..	..	*21*	*21*	..
Baroda State	16	15	1	16	15	1	..	..	..	..	..	..
Bengal States	7	6	1	7	6	1	..	..	..	..	..	..
Bombay States	68	61	7	57	50	7	..	..	..	11	11	..
Central India (*Agency*).	53	53	..	52	52	..	..	..	..	1	1	..
Central Provinces States	6	6	..	6	6	..	..	..	..	..	..	..
Gwalior State	95	95	..	93	93	..	..	..	..	2	2	..
Hyderabad State	44	39	5	43	38	5	..	..	..	1	1	..
Kashmir State	2	2	..	2	2	..	..	..	..	..	..	..
Madras States	46	46	..	46	46	..	..	..	..	..	..	..
Cochin State	*23*	*23*	..	*23*	*23*	..	..	..	..	..	..	..
Travancore State	*21*	*21*	..	*21*	*21*	..	..	..	..	..	..	..
Mysore State	71	67	4	71	67	4	..	..	..	..	..	..
Punjab States	66	66	..	66	66	..	..	..	..	..	..	..
Rajputana (*Agency*)	175	173	2	170	168	2	..	..	..	5	5	..
United Provinces States	11	1	10	10	..	10	..	..	..	1	1	..
(c) *India, Unspecified*	*234*	*210*	*24*	*174*	*150*	*24*	*60*	*60*	..	..	..	..
(d) *French and Portuguese Settlements.*	*88*	*86*	*2*	*86*	*84*	*2*	*2*	*2*	..	..	..	..
B.—Born in other Asiatic Countries.	***564***	***558***	***6***	***242***	***239***	***3***	***1***	***1***	..	***321***	***318***	***3***
Afghanistan	9	9	..	9	9	..	..	..	..	..	..	..
Bhotan	13	13	..	13	13	..	..	..	..	..	..	..
Ceylon	73	72	1	71	70	1	1	1	..	1	1	..
China	428	425	3	108	108	..	..	..	..	320	317	3
Hongkong	8	6	2	8	6	2	..	..	..	..	..	..
Japan	3	3	..	3	3	..	..	..	..	..	..	..
Nepal	10	10	..	10	10	..	..	..	..	..	..	..
Siam	7	7	..	7	7	..	..	..	..	..	..	..
Straits Settlements	12	12	..	12	12	..	..	..	..	..	..	..
Turkey in Asia	1	1	..	1	1	..	..	..	..	..	..	..
C.—Born in Europe.	***139***	***124***	***15***	***96***	***81***	***15***	***43***	***43***	..	..	..	..
United Kingdom	133	121	12	90	78	12	43	43	..	..	..	..
England and Wales	*69*	*58*	*11*	*46*	*35*	*11*	*23*	*23*	..	..	..	..
Scotland	*59*	*59*	..	*39*	*39*	..	*20*	*20*	..	..	..	..
Ireland	*5*	*4*	*1*	*5*	*4*	*1*	..	..	..	..	..	..
France	1	1	..	1	1	..	..	..	..	..	..	..
Germany	1	1	..	1	1	..	..	..	..	..	..	..
Italy	1	1	..	1	1	..	..	..	..	..	..	..
Russia	1	..	1	1	..	1	..	..	..	..	..	..
Europe, Unspecified	2	..	2	2	..	2	..	..	..	..	..	..
D.—Born in Africa (Egypt).	***1***	***1***	..	..	..	..	..	..	..	***1***	***1***	..
E.—Born in America (unspecified)	***5***	***5***	..	***2***	***2***	..	.	..	..	***3***	***3***	..
F.—Born in Australasia (Borneo).	***15***	***15***	..	***15***	***15***	..	..	..	..	..	..	..

TABLE XII—Infirmities. Part I.—Distribution by age.

Note.—The age periods in which there are no infirmities have been omitted.

Age.	Population Afflicted.			Insane.			Deaf-mutes.			Blind.			Lepers.		
	Persons.	Males.	Females.	Persons.	Males.	Females.	Persons.	Males.	Females.	Persons.	Males.	Females.	Persons.	Males.	Females.
1	2	3	4	5	6	7	8	9	10	11	12	13	14	15	16
TOTAL	**65**	**59**	**6**	**34**	**31**	**3**	**2**	**1**	**1**	**5**	**3**	**2**	**24**	**24**	...
15—20	1	...	1	...	...	...	1	...	1	...	...	...	...	...	...
20—25	2	2	...	1	1	...	1	1	...	...	...	...	...	...	...
25—30	9	9	...	6	6	...	...	...	...	...	...	...	3	3	...
30—35	11	9	2	8	6	2	...	...	...	1	1	...	2	2	...
35—40	6	6	...	3	3	...	...	...	...	...	...	...	3	3	...
40—45	13	11	2	8	7	1	...	...	...	1	...	1	4	4	...
45—50	12	12	...	6	6	...	...	...	...	1	1	...	5	5	...
50—55	9	8	1	2	2	...	...	...	...	2	1	1	5	5	...
55—60	1	1	...	...	...	...	...	...	...	...	...	...	1	1	...
60—65	1	1	...	...	...	...	...	...	...	...	...	...	1	1	...

TABLE XII.—Infirmities. Part II.—Distribution by Locality.

Locality.	Population Afflicted.			Insane.			Deaf-Mutes.			Blind.			Lepers.		
	Persons.	Males.	Females.	Persons.	Males.	Females.	Persons.	Males.	Females.	Persons.	Males.	Females.	Persons.	Males.	Females.
1	2	3	4	5	6	7	8	9	10	11	12	13	14	15	16
Andamans and Nicobars	**65**	**59**	**6**	**34**	**31**	**3**	**2**	**1**	**1**	**5**	**3**	**2**	**24**	**24**	...
Port Blair	58	55	3	32	29	3	...	...	...	2	2	...	24	24	...
Nicobars	7	4	3	2	2	...	2	1	1	3	1	2	...	...	...

TABLE XII-A.—Infirmities by Selected Castes, Tribes or Races.

Caste, Tribe or Race.	Population dealt with.			Insane.		Deaf-mutes.		Blind.		Lepers.	
	Persons.	Males.	Females.	Males.	Females.	Males.	Females.	Males.	Females.	Males.	Females.
1	2	3	4	5	6	7	8	9	10	11	12
Ahir	390	338	52	...	...	...	...	...	1	...	...
Bhangi	110	94	16	1	...	...	...	...	...	...	...
Biloch	86	86	...	3	...	...	...	...	...	1	...
Brahman	746	633	113	3	...	...	...	...	...	4	...
Chamar	301	232	69	3	...	...	...	...	...	...	...
Jat	482	452	30	1	1	...	...	...	...	2	...
Kayastha	172	117	55	2	...	...	...	...	...	...	...
Kori	101	73	28	1	...	...	...	...	...	2	...
Kurmi	526	374	152	...	...	...	...	...	...	1	...
Lodha	89	77	12	1	...	...	...	...	...	...	...
Nai	172	143	29	1	1	...	...	...	...	...	...
Nicobarese	8,244	4,439	3,805	...	...	1	...	1	1	...	...
Pathan	635	611	24	1	...	...	...	...	...	...	...
Rajput	1,124	981	143	1	...	...	...	...	...	1	...
Sheikh	1,583	1,312	271	3	1	...	...	...	...	3	...
Sunar	89	70	19	...	...	...	...	...	...	1	...
Teli	155	113	42	...	...	...	...	...	...	2	...

TABLE XIII.—Caste, Tribe, Race or Nationality.

The estimated population noted below is excluded from this table.

	Males.	Females.
Andamanese	310	267
Nicobarese	190	185

2. The figures for Christians are omitted from this Table as they are specially dealt with in Tables XV and XVI.

Caste, Tribe, Race or Nationality.	Andamans and Nicobars.		Port Blair.		Rest of Andamans.		Nicobars.	
	Males.	Females.	Males.	Females.	Males.	Females.	Males.	Females.
1	2	3	4	5	6	7	8	9
All Castes	**18,832**	**5,716**	**13,450**	**1,847**	**367**	**48**	**5,015**	**3,821**
Agarwal	60	18	60	16	...	2	...	...
Hindu	58	18	58	16	...	2	...	...
Arya	2	...	2	...	...	...	...	...
Ahar	50	38	50	34	...	4	...	...
Hindu	47	38	47	34	...	4	...	...
Arya	3	...	3	...	...	...	...	...
Ahir (*Hindu*)	338	52	334	52	4	...	...	...
Baniya (*Hindu*)	25	6	20	6	5	...	...	...
Bhangi	94	16	89	13	5	3	...	...
Hindu	89	13	84	10	5	3	...	...
Sikh	1	...	1	...	...	...	...	...
Musalman	4	3	4	3	...	...	...	...
Biloch (*Musalman*)	86	...	86	...	...	...	...	...
Brahman	633	113	626	110	6	3	1	...
Hindu	614	110	610	107	3	3	1	...
Arya	11	...	11	...	...	...	...	...
Sikh	5	3	5	3	...	...	...	...
Buddhist	3	...	...	...	3	...	...	...
Burmese	2,398	66	2,251	43	80	11	67	12
Hindu	6	...	6	...	...	...	...	...
Arya	1	...	1	...	...	...	...	...
Buddhist	2,391	66	2,244	43	80	11	67	12
Chamar	232	69	227	69	5	...	...	...
Hindu	231	68	226	68	5	...	...	...
Arya	1	...	1	...	...	...	...	...
Buddhist	...	1	...	1	...	...	...	...
Gond (*Hindu*)	157	19	157	19	...	...	...	...
Jat	452	30	452	30	...	...	...	...
Hindu	97	5	97	5	...	...	...	...
Arya	2	...	2	...	...	...	...	...
Sikh	289	18	289	18	...	...	...	...
Musalman	64	7	64	7	...	...	...	...
Kachhi	115	59	112	54	3	5	...	...
Hindu	109	58	106	53	3	5	...	...
Musalman	6	1	6	1	...	...	...	...
Kahar	175	40	175	40	...	...	...	...
Hindu	137	38	137	38	...	...	...	...
Arya	2	...	2	...	...	...	...	...
Sikh	11	2	11	2	...	...	...	...
Musalman	25	...	25	...	...	...	...	...
Kayastha	117	55	111	52	5	3	1	...
Hindu	116	55	110	52	5	3	1	...
Arya	1	...	1	...	...	...	...	...
Kori (*Hindu*)	73	28	72	28	1	...	...	...

TABLE XIII.—Caste, Tribe, Race or Nationality—*contd.*

Caste, Tribe, Race or Nationality.	Andamans and Nicobars.		Port Blair.		Rest of Andamans.		Nicobars.	
	Males.	Females.	Males.	Females.	Males.	Females.	Males.	Females.
1	2	3	4	5	6	7	8	9
Kurmi	374	152	361	147	13	5	...	...
Hindu	373	152	360	147	13	5	...	...
Arya	1	...	1	...	...	...	...	...
Lodha	77	12	77	12	...	...	...	...
Hindu	75	12	75	12	...	...	...	...
Sikh	2	...	2	...	...	...	...	...
Mahesri (*Hindu*)	10	...	10	...	...	...	...	...
Maratha (*Hindu*)	80	10	79	9	1	1	...	...
Nai	143	29	142	29	...	...	1	...
Hindu	102	28	101	28	...	...	1	...
Arya	1	...	1	...	...	...	...	...
Sikh	16	...	16	...	...	...	...	...
Musalman	24	1	24	1	...	...	...	...
Nicobarese	4,439	3,805	...	...	...	...	4,439	3,805
Buddhist	16	...	...	...	...	...	16	...
Animist	4,417	3,805	...	...	...	...	4,417	3,805
Confucian	6	...	...	...	...	...	6	...
Pasi (*Hindu*)	211	15	209	15	2	...	...	...
Pathan (*Musalman*)	611	24	605	23	6	1	...	...
Rajput	981	143	962	143	12	...	7	...
Hindu	821	127	808	127	12	...	1	...
Arya	8	1	8	1	...	...	...	...
Sikh	5	...	5	...	...	...	...	...
Musalman	147	15	141	15	...	...	6	...
Rangrez (*Musalman*)	2	2	2	2	...	...	...	...
Saiyad (*Musalman*)	129	26	122	26	7	...	...	...
Sheikh (*Musalman*)	1,312	271	1,256	265	53	6	3	...
Sunar	70	19	70	19	...	...	...	...
Hindu	57	16	57	16	...	...	...	...
Sikh	1	...	1	...	...	...	...	...
Musalman	12	3	12	3	...	...	...	...
Teli	113	42	113	42	...	...	...	...
Hindu	79	37	79	37	...	...	...	...
Musalman	34	5	34	5	...	...	...	...
Others	5,275	557	4,620	549	159	4	496	4
Hindu	3,550	454	3,425	453	123	1	2	...
Arya	32	...	32	...	...	...	...	...
Sikh	36	1	33	1	...	...	3	...
Buddhist	170	5	117	...	35	3	18	2
Musalman	1,194	96	1,013	95	1	...	180	1
Confucian	293	1	...	...	...	...	293	1

TABLE XV.—Christians by Sect and Race.

Locality.	All Denominations. Total. P.	Total. M.	Total. F.	European and Allied Races. M.	European and Allied Races. F.	Anglo-Indian. M.	Anglo-Indian. F.	Indian. M.	Indian. F.	Anglican Communion. Total. P.	Total. M.	Total. F.	European and Allied Races. M.	European and Allied Races. F.	Anglo-Indian. M.	Anglo-Indian. F.	Indian. M.	Indian. F.
1	2	3	4	5	6	7	8	9	10	11	12	13	14	15	16	17	18	19
ANDAMANS AND NICOBARS.	1,586	1,461	125	171	38	15	10	1,275	77	128	85	43	50	24	..	3	35	16
Port Blair	378	297	81	168	36	8	8	121	37	78	51	27	50	24	..	3	1	..
Rest of Andamans	1,147	1,127	20	3	2	7	2	1,117	16	..	..	..	..	..	..	..	..	..
Nicobars	61	37	24	..	..	..	..	37	24	50	34	16	..	..	..	..	34	16

Locality.	Baptist. Total. P.	Total. M.	Total. F.	European and Allied Races. M.	European and Allied Races. F.	Anglo-Indian. M.	Anglo-Indian. F.	Indian. M.	Indian. F.	Protestants (Unsectarian or Sect not specified). Total. P.	Total. M.	Total. F.	European and Allied Races. M.	European and Allied Races. F.	Anglo-Indian. M.	Anglo-Indian. F.	Indian. M.	Indian. F.
1	20	21	22	23	24	25	26	27	28	29	30	31	32	33	34	35	36	37
ANDAMANS AND NICOBARS.	3	..	3	..	..	..	3	..	..	58	45	13	20	..	2	2	23	11
Port Blair	2	..	2	..	..	..	2	..	..	58	45	13	20	..	2	2	23	11
Rest of Andamans	1	..	1	..	..	..	1	..	..	..	..	..	..	..	..	..	..	..
Nicobars	..	..	..	..	..	..	..	..	..	..	..	..	..	..	..	..	..	..

Locality.	Roman Catholic. Total. P.	Total. M.	Total. F.	European and Allied Races. M.	European and Allied Races. F.	Anglo-Indian. M.	Anglo-Indian. F.	Indian. M.	Indian. F.
1	38	39	40	41	42	43	44	45	46
ANDAMANS AND NICOBARS.	1,397	1,331	66	101	14	13	2	1,217	50
Port Blair	240	201	39	98	12	6	1	97	26
Rest of Andamans	1,146	1,127	19	3	2	7	1	1,117	16
Nicobars	11	3	8	..	..	..	..	3	8

TABLE XVI.—European and Allied Races and Anglo-Indians by Race and Age.

(a) *European and Allied Races.*

Locality.	TOTAL.			British Subjects.																		Others.																	
				All Ages.			0—10		10—16		16—18		18—30		30—40		40—50		50 and over			All Ages			0—10		10—16		16—18		18—30		30—40		40—50		50 and over.	
	Total.	Males.	Females.	Total.	Males.	Females.	Males.	Females.	Males.	Females.	Males.	Females.	Males.	Females.	Males.	Females.	Males.	Females.	Males.	Females.	Total.	Males.	Females.	Males.	Females.	Males.	Females.	Males.	Females.	Males.	Females.	Males.	Females.	Males.	Females.	Males.	Females.
1	2	3	4	5	6	7	8	9	10	11	12	13	14	15	16	17	18	19	20	21	22	23	24	25	26	27	28	29	30	31	32	33	34	35	36	37	38
Andamans and Nicobars	209	171	38	209	171	38	9	7	1	2	..	..	89	8	39	13	16	8	17	..	..	..	..	..	..	..	..	..	..	..	..	..	..	..	..	..	..
Port Blair	204	168	36	204	168	36	8	7	1	2	..	..	89	8	38	11	16	8	16	..	..	..	..	..	..	..	..	..	..	..	..	..	..	..	..	..	..
Rest of Andamans	5	3	2	5	3	2	1	..	..	..	..	..	..	..	1	2	..	..	1	..	..	..	..	..	..	..	..	..	..	..	..	..	..	..	..	..	..
Nicobars	..	..	..	..	..	..	..	..	..	..	..	..	..	..	..	..	..	..	..	..	..	..	..	..	..	..	..	..	..	..	..	..	..	..	..	..	..

(b) *Anglo-Indian.*

Locality.	All Ages.			0—1		1—5		5—10		10—15		15—20		20—30		30—40		40—50		50—60		60 and over		16—18		18—20	
	Total.	Males.	Females.	Males.	Females.	Males.	Females.	Males.	Females.	Males.	Females.	Males.	Females.	Males.	Females.	Males.	Females.	Males.	Females.	Males.	Females.	Males.	Females.	Males.	Females.	Males.	Females.
1	2	3	4	5	6	7	8	9	10	11	12	13	14	15	16	17	18	19	20	21	22	23	24	25	26	27	28
Andamans and Nicobars	25	15	10	..	..	..	..	1	1	1	3	1	..	4	2	6	..	2	3	..	1	..	..	1	..	..	..
Port Blair	16	8	8	..	..	..	..	1	1	1	2	1	..	..	1	3	..	2	3	..	1	..	..	1	..	..	..
Rest of Andamans	9	7	2	..	..	..	..	..	..	..	1	..	..	4	1	3	..	..	..	..	..	..	..	..	..	..	..
Nicobars	..	..	..	..	..	..	..	..	..	..	..	..	..	..	..	..	..	..	..	..	..	..	..	..	..	..	..

TABLE XVII.—OCCUPATION OR MEANS OF LIVELIHOOD.—GENERAL TABLE.

NOTES—1. The estimated Andamanese (577) and Nicobarese (375) are omitted from this Table.
2. Blank Groups have been omitted.

Group number.	Occupation or means of livelihood.	ANDAMANS AND NICOBARS.						PORT BLAIR.						REST OF ANDAMANS.						NICOBARS.					
		Total workers and dependants.	ACTUAL WORKERS.				Dependants.	Total workers and dependants.	ACTUAL WORKERS.				Dependants.	Total workers and dependants.	ACTUAL WORKERS.				Dependants.	Total workers and dependants.	ACTUAL WORKERS.				Dependants.
			Total.		Partially agriculturists.				Total.		Partially agriculturists.				Total.		Partially agriculturists.				Total		Partially agriculturists.		
			Males.	Females	Males.	Females			Males.	Females	Males.	Females			Males.	Females	Males.	Females			Males.	Females	Males.	Females	
1	2	3	4	5	6	7	8	9	10	11	12	13	14	15	16	17	18	19	20	21	22	23	24	25	26
	Andamans and Nicobars	**26,134**	**17,881**	**2,906**	**312**	**1**	**5,347**	**15,675**	**12,936**	**482**	**29**	**1**	**2,257**	**1,562**	**1,473**	**27**	**283**	...	**62**	**5,897**	**3,472**	**2,397**	...	...	**3,028**
	A.—Production of raw materials.	*10,801*	*4,199*	*2,456*	*257*	..	*4,146*	*1,597*	*412*	*50*	*7*	..	*1,135*	*914*	*886*	*18*	*250*	..	*10*	*8,290*	*2,901*	*2,388*	..	..	*3,001*
	I.—EXPLOITATION OF ANIMALS AND VEGETATION.	10,801	4,199	2,456	257	..	4,146	1,597	412	50	7	..	1,135	914	886	18	250	..	10	8,290	2,901	2,388	..	..	3,001
	1.—Pasture and Agriculture	10,794	4,196	2,455	257	..	4,143	1,590	409	49	7	..	1,132	914	886	18	250	..	10	8,290	2,901	2,388	..	..	3,001
	(a) Ordinary Cultivation	9,835	3,681	2,334	..	..	3,820	1,506	374	31	..	..	1,101	600	573	17	..	..	10	7,729	2,734	2,286	..	..	2,709
1	Income from rent of Agricultural land.	159	158	1	..	..	..	16	16	..	..	..	..	143	142	1	..	..	..	..	..	..	..	..	..
2	Ordinary cultivators	9,668	3,523	2,333	..	..	3,812	1,482	358	31	..	..	1,093	457	431	16	..	..	10	7,729	2,734	2,286	..	..	2,709
3	Agents, managers of landed estates (not planters), clerks, rent collectors, etc.	8	..	..	..	..	8	8	..	..	..	..	8	..	..	..	..	..	..	..	..	..	..	..	..
	(b) Growers of special products and market gardening.	588	174	109	..	..	305	29	..	7	..	..	13	7	7	..	..	..	..	561	167	102	..	..	292
7	Fruit, flower, vegetable, betel, vine, areca nut, etc., growers.	588	174	109	..	..	305	20	..	7	..	..	13	7	7	..	..	..	..	561	167	102	..	..	292
	(c) Forestry	356	327	11	257	..	18	49	21	10	7	..	18	307	306	1	250	..	..	..	..	..	..	..	..
8	Forest officers, rangers, guards, etc.	350	321	11	257	..	18	49	21	10	7	..	18	301	300	1	250	..	..	..	..	..	..	..	..
9	Wood-cutters, firewood, catechu, rubber, etc., collectors, and charcoal burners.	6	6	..	..	..	..	..	..	..	..	..	..	6	6	..	..	..	..	..	..	..	..	..	..
	(d) Raising of farm-stock	14	14	..	..	..	..	14	14	..	..	..	..	..	..	..	..	..	..	..	..	..	..	..	..
14	Herdsmen, shepherds, goatherds, etc.	14	14	..	..	..	..	14	14	..	..	..	..	..	..	..	..	..	..	..	..	..	..	..	..
	(e) Raising of small animals	1	..	1	..	..	..	1	..	1	..	..	..	..	..	..	..	..	..	..	..	..	..	..	..
15	Birds, bees, etc.	1	..	1	..	..	..	1	..	1	..	..	..	..	..	..	..	..	..	..	..	..	..	..	..
	2.—Fishing and Hunting	7	3	1	..	..	..	7	3	1	..	..	3	..	..	..	..	..	..	..	..	..	..	..	..
17	Fishing	7	3	1	..	..	..	7	3	1	..	..	3	..	..	..	..	..	..	..	..	..	..	..	..

	B.—Preparation and supply of material substances.	*1,157*	*723*	*40*	*2*	..	*394*	*573*	*173*	*34*	*2*	..	*366*	*50*	*41*	*1*	..	..	*8*	*534*	*509*	*5*	..	..	*20*
	III.—INDUSTRY	223	110	10	1	..	103	169	65	9	1	..	95	49	40	1	..	..	8	5	5	..	..	..	..
	6.—Textiles	17	9	..	..	..	8	16	9	..	..	..	7	1	..	..	..	..	1	..	..	..	..	..	..
27	Cotton sizing and weaving.	17	9	..	..	..	8	16	9	..	..	..	7	1	..	..	..	..	1	..	..	..	..	..	..
	8.—Wood	99	60	..	1	..	39	55	22	..	1	..	33	43	37	..	..	..	6	1	1	..	..	..	..
43	Sawyers	29	7	..	..	..	22	23	7	..	..	..	16	6	..	..	..	..	6	..	..	..	..	..	..
44	Carpenters, turners and joiners, etc.	55	49	..	1	..	6	17	11	..	1	..	6	37	37	..	..	..	..	1	1	..	..	..	..
45	Basket makers and other industries of woody material, including leaves and thatchers and builders working with bamboo, reeds or similar materials.	15	4	..	..	..	11	15	4	..	..	..	11	..	..	..	..	..	..	..	..	..	..	..	..
	12.—Food industries	26	3	7	..	..	16	26	3	7	..	..	16	..	..	..	..	..	..	..	..	..	..	..	..
65	Rice pounders and huskers and flour grinders.	7	..	6	..	..	1	7	..	6	..	..	1	..	..	..	..	..	..	..	..	..	..	..	..
66	Bakers and biscuit makers.	11	..	1	..	..	10	11	..	1	..	..	10	..	..	..	..	..	..	..	..	..	..	..	..
67	Grain parchers, etc.	5	3	..	..	..	2	5	3	..	..	..	2	..	..	..	..	..	..	..	..	..	..	..	..
74	Toddy drawers	3	..	..	..	..	3	3	..	..	..	..	3	..	..	..	..	..	..	..	..	..	..	..	..
	13.—Industries of dress and the toilet.	39	17	1	..	..	21	36	15	..	..	..	21	3	2	1	..	..	..	..	..	..	..	..	..
77	Tailors, milliners, dress makers, darners and embroiderers on linen.	21	8	..	..	..	13	21	8	..	..	..	13	..	..	..	..	..	..	..	..	..	..	..	..
78	Shoe, boot and sandal makers.	3	2	..	..	..	1	1	..	..	..	..	1	2	2	..	..	..	..	..	..	..	..	..	..
80	Washing, cleaning and dyeing.	4	1	1	..	..	2	3	1	..	..	..	2	1	..	1	..	..	..	..	..	..	..	..	..
81	Barbers, hairdressers and wig makers.	11	6	..	..	..	5	11	6	..	..	..	5	..	..	..	..	..	..	..	..	..	..	..	..
	17.—Production and transmission of physical forces (heat, light, electricity, motive power, etc.)	2	..	..	..	..	2	2	..	..	..	..	2	..	..	..	..	..	..	..	..	..	..	..	..
93	Gas works and electric light and power.	2	..	..	..	..	2	2	..	..	..	..	2	..	..	..	..	..	..	..	..	..	..	..	..
	18.—Other miscellaneous and undefined industries.	40	21	2	..	..	17	34	16	2	..	..	16	2	1	..	..	..	1	4	4	..	..	..	..
94	Printers, lithographers, engravers, etc.	2	2	..	..	..	..	2	2	..	..	..	..	..	..	..	..	..	..	..	..	..	..	..	..
98	Workers in precious stones and metals, enamellers, imitation jewellery makers, gilders, etc.	23	10	2	..	..	11	23	10	2	..	..	11	..	..	..	..	..	..	..	..	..	..	..	..

TABLE XVII.—OCCUPATION OR MEANS OF LIVELIHOOD—GENERAL TABLE—*continued*.

Group Number.	Occupation or means of livelihood.	ANDAMANS AND NICOBARS. Total workers and dependants.	Actual workers. Total. Males.	Actual workers. Total. Females.	Actual workers. Partially agriculturists. Males.	Actual workers. Partially agriculturists. Females.	Dependants.	PORT BLAIR. Total workers and dependants.	Actual workers. Total. Males.	Actual workers. Total. Females.	Actual workers. Partially agriculturists. Males.	Actual workers. Partially agriculturists. Females.	Dependants.	REST OF ANDAMANS. Total workers and dependants.	Actual workers. Total. Males.	Actual workers. Total. Females.	Actual workers. Partially agriculturists. Males.	Actual workers. Partially agriculturists. Females.	Dependants.	NICOBARS. Total workers and dependants.	Actual workers. Total. Males.	Actual workers. Total. Females.	Actual workers. Partially agriculturists. Males.	Actual workers. Partially agriculturists. Females.	Dependants.
1	2	3	4	5	6	7	8	9	10	11	12	13	14	15	16	17	18	19	20	21	22	23	24	25	26
	18.—Other miscellaneous and undefined industries—*continued*.																								
101	Others, including managers, persons (other than performers) employed in theatres and other places of public entertainment, employés of public societies, race course service, huntsmen, etc.	2	..	..	..	..	2	2	..	..	..	..	2	..	..	..	..	..	..	..	..	..	..	..	..
103	Sweepers, scavengers, etc.	13	9	..	..	..	4	7	4	..	..	..	3	2	1	..	..	..	1	4	4	..	..	..	..
	IV.—TRANSPORT	175	103	1	1	..	71	100	28	1	1	..	71	..	..	..	..	..	..	75	75	..	..	..	..
	20.—Transport by water	93	83	..	..	..	10	19	9	..	..	..	10	..	..	..	..	..	..	74	74	..	..	..	..
105	Persons (other than labourers) employed in harbours and docks including pilots.	8	6	..	..	..	2	8	6	..	..	..	2	..	..	..	..	..	..	..	..	..	..	..	..
107	Ship owners and their employés, ship brokers, ships' officers, engineers, mariners and firemen.	85	77	..	..	..	8	11	3	..	..	..	8	..	..	..	..	..	..	74	74	..	..	..	..
	21.—Transport by road	16	5	..	1	..	11	15	4	..	1	..	11	..	..	..	..	..	..	1	1	..	..	..	..
114	Owners, managers and employés (excluding personal servants) connected with vehicles other than those driven mechanically.	4	3	..	..	..	1	3	2	..	..	..	1	..	..	..	..	..	..	1	1	..	..	..	..
117	Porters and messengers	12	2	..	1	..	10	12	2	..	1	..	10	..	..	..	..	..	..	..	..	..	..	..	..
	22.—Transport by rail	34	6	..	..	..	28	34	6	..	..	..	28	..	..	..	..	..	..	..	..	..	..	..	..
118	Railway employés of all kinds other than coolies.	34	6	..	..	..	28	34	6	..	..	..	28	..	..	..	..	..	..	..	..	..	..	..	..
	23.—Post Office, Telegraph and Telephone services.	32	9	1	..	..	22	32	9	1	..	..	22	..	..	..	..	..	..	..	..	..	..	..	..
120	Post Office, Telegraph and Telephone services.	32	9	1	..	..	22	32	9	1	..	..	22	..	..	..	..	..	..	..	..	..	..	..	..

	V.—TRADE	759	510	29	..	..	200	304	80	24	..	..	200	1	1	..	..	..	..	454	429	5	..	..	20
	24.—Banks, establishments of credit, exchange and insurance.	2	1	..	..	..	1	2	1	..	..	..	1	..	..	..	..	..	..	..	..	..	..	..	..
121	Bank managers, money-lenders, exchange and insurance agents, money changers and brokers and their employés.	2	1	..	..	..	1	2	1	..	..	..	1	..	..	..	..	..	..	..	..	..	..	..	..
	25.—Brokerage, commission and export.	9	9	..	..	..	..	9	9	..	..	..	..	..	..	..	..	..	..	..	..	..	..	..	..
122	Brokers, commission agents, commercial travellers, warehouse owners and employés.	9	9	..	..	..	..	9	9	..	..	..	..	..	..	..	..	..	..	..	..	..	..	..	..
	31.—Trade in chemical products.	17	..	..	..	..	17	17	..	..	..	..	17	..	..	..	..	..	..	..	..	..	..	..	..
128	Trade in chemical products, (drugs, dyes, paints, petroleum, explosives, etc.)	17	..	..	..	..	17	17	..	..	..	..	17	..	..	..	..	..	..	..	..	..	..	..	..
	33.—Other trade in food-stuffs.	371	264	25	..	..	82	133	32	20	..	..	81	..	..	..	..	..	..	238	232	5	..	..	1
132	Grocers and sellers of vegetable oil, salt and other condiments.	14	5	..	..	..	9	14	5	..	..	..	9	..	..	..	..	..	..	..	..	..	..	..	..
133	Sellers of milk, butter, ghee, poultry, eggs, etc.	65	13	13	..	..	39	65	13	13	..	..	39	..	..	..	..	..	..	..	..	..	..	..	..
134	Sellers of sweetmeats, sugar, gur and molasses.	30	9	1	..	..	20	30	9	1	..	..	20	..	..	..	..	..	..	..	..	..	..	..	..
135	Cardamom, betel-leaf, vegetables, fruit and areca nut sellers.	253	237	6	..	..	10	15	5	1	..	..	9	..	..	..	..	..	..	238	232	5	..	..	1
136	Grain and pulse dealers	9	..	5	..	..	4	9	..	5	..	..	4	..	..	..	..	..	..	..	..	..	..	..	..
	34.—Trade in clothing and toilet articles.	53	..	..	..	..	53	53	..	..	..	..	53	..	..	..	..	..	..	..	..	..	..	..	..
140	Trade in ready-made clothing and other articles of dress and the toilet (hats, umbrellas, socks, ready-made shoes, perfumes, etc.)	53	..	..	..	..	53	53	..	..	..	..	53	..	..	..	..	..	..	..	..	..	..	..	..
	40.—Trade of other sorts.	307	236	4	..	..	67	90	38	4	..	..	48	1	1	..	..	..	..	216	197	..	..	..	19
152	General store-keepers and shop-keepers otherwise unspecified.	307	236	4	..	..	67	90	38	4	..	..	48	1	1	..	..	..	..	216	197	..	..	..	19
	C.—Public administration and liberal arts.	*1,856*	*1,276*	*18*	*13*	*1*	*562*	*1,753*	*1,211*	*13*	*13*	*1*	*529*	*87*	*60*	*1*	..	..	*26*	*16*	*5*	*4*	..	..	*7*
	VI.—PUBLIC FORCE . .	1,005	777	..	..	..	228	997	773	..	..	..	224	5	1	..	..	..	4	3	3	..	..	..	..
	41.—Army . . .	672	508	..	..	..	164	672	508	..	..	..	164	..	..	..	..	..	..	..	..	..	..	..	..
155	Army (Imperial) . .	672	508	..	..	..	164	672	508	..	..	..	164	..	..	..	..	..	..	..	..	..	..	..	..

TABLE XVII.—OCCUPATION OR MEANS OF LIVELIHOOD—GENERAL TABLE.—*concluded.*

Group Number	Occupation or means of livelihood.	ANDAMANS AND NICOBARS. Total workers and dependants.	Actual workers. Total. Males.	Actual workers. Total. Females.	Actual workers. Partially agriculturists. Males.	Actual workers. Partially agriculturists. Females.	Dependants.	PORT BLAIR. Total workers and dependants.	Actual workers. Total. Males.	Actual workers. Total. Females.	Actual workers. Partially agriculturists. Males.	Actual workers. Partially agriculturists. Females.	Dependants.	REST OF ANDAMANS. Total workers and dependants.	Actual workers. Total. Males.	Actual workers. Total. Females.	Actual workers. Partially agriculturists. Males.	Actual workers. Partially agriculturists. Females.	Dependants.	NICOBARS. Total workers and dependants.	Actual workers. Total. Males.	Actual workers. Total. Females.	Actual workers. Partially agriculturists. Males.	Actual workers. Partially agriculturists. Females.	Dependants.
1	2	3	4	5	6	7	8	9	10	11	12	13	14	15	16	17	18	19	20	21	22	23	24	25	26
	42.—Navy	2	1	..	..	..	1	2	1	..	..	..	1	..	..	..	..	..	..	..	..	..	..	..	..
157	Navy	2	1	..	..	..	1	2	1	..	..	..	1	..	..	..	..	..	..	..	..	..	..	..	..
	44.—Police	331	268	..	..	..	63	323	264	..	..	..	59	5	1	..	..	..	4	3	3	..	..	..	..
159	Police	283	253	..	..	..	30	279	249	..	..	..	30	1	1	..	..	..	..	3	3	..	..	..	..
160	Village watchmen	48	15	..	..	..	33	44	15	..	..	..	29	4	..	..	..	..	4	..	..	..	..	..	..
	VII.—PUBLIC ADMINISTRATION.	549	245	13	..	..	291	470	187	12	..	..	271	77	57	1	..	..	19	2	1	..	..	..	1
	45.—Public Administration	549	245	13	..	..	291	470	187	12	..	..	271	77	57	1	..	..	19	2	1	..	..	..	1
161	Service of the State	546	244	13	..	..	289	467	186	12	..	..	269	77	57	1	..	..	19	2	1	..	..	..	1
164	Village officials and servants other than watchmen.	3	1	..	..	..	2	3	1	..	..	..	2	..	..	..	..	..	..	..	..	..	..	..	..
	VIII.—PROFESSIONS AND LIBERAL ARTS.	302	254	5	13	1	43	286	251	1	13	1	34	5	2	..	..	..	3	11	1	4	..	..	6
	46.—Religion	34	32	1	13	1	1	34	32	1	13	1	1	..	..	..	..	..	..	..	..	..	..	..	..
165	Priests, ministers, etc.	2	2	..	..	..	..	2	2	..	..	..	..	..	..	..	..	..	..	..	..	..	..	..	..
166	Religious mendicants, inmates of monasteries, etc.	32	30	1	13	1	1	32	30	1	13	1	1	..	..	..	..	..	..	..	..	..	..	..	..
	47.—Law	3	2	..	..	..	1	3	2	..	..	..	1	..	..	..	..	..	..	..	..	..	..	..	..
170	Lawyers' clerks, petition writers, etc.	3	2	..	..	..	1	3	2	..	..	..	1	..	..	..	..	..	..	..	..	..	..	..	..
	48.—Medicine	224	202	4	..	..	18	210	201	..	..	..	9	4	1	..	..	..	3	10	..	4	..	..	6
171	Medical practitioners of all kinds, including dentists, oculists and veterinary surgeons.	192	180	4	..	..	8	182	180	..	..	..	2	..	..	..	..	..	..	10	..	4	..	..	6
172	Midwives, vaccinators, compounders, nurses, masseurs, etc.	32	22	..	..	..	10	28	21	..	..	..	7	4	1	..	..	..	3	..	..	..	..	..	..
	49.—Instruction	24	12	..	..	..	12	22	10	..	..	..	12	1	1	..	..	..	..	1	1	..	..	..	..
173	Professors and teachers of all kinds.	10	1	..	..	..	9	9	..	..	..	..	9	..	..	..	..	..	..	1	1	..	..	..	..
174	Clerks and servants connected with education.	14	11	..	..	..	3	13	10	..	..	..	3	1	1	..	..	..	..	..	..	..	..	..	..

	50.—Letters and arts and sciences.	17	6	..	..	..	11	17	6	..	..	..	11	..	..	..	..	..	..	..	..	..	..	..	..
176	Architects, surveyors, engineers, and their employés.	17	6	..	..	..	11	17	6	..	..	..	11	..	..	..	..	..	..	..	..	..	..	..	..
	D.—Miscellaneous . .	*12,390*	*11,683*	*392*	*40*	..	*245*	*11,753*	*11,140*	*385*	*7*	..	*227*	*511*	*486*	*7*	*33*	..	*18*	*57*	*57*	..	..	..	..
	IX.—PERSONS LIVING ON THEIR INCOME.	17	3	5	..	..	9	17	3	5	..	..	9	..	..	..	..	..	..	..	..	..	..	..	..
	51.—Persons living principally on their income.	17	3	5	..	..	9	17	3	5	..	..	9	..	..	..	..	..	..	..	..	..	..	..	..
180	Proprietors (other than agricultural land), fund and scholarship holders and pensioners.	17	3	5	..	..	9	17	3	5	..	..	9	..	..	..	..	..	..	..	..	..	..	..	..
	X.—DOMESTIC SERVICE .	213	132	8	1	..	73	137	69	7	1	..	61	69	56	1	..	..	12	7	7	..	..	..	..
	52.—Domestic service .	213	132	8	1	..	73	137	69	7	1	..	61	69	56	1	..	..	12	7	7	..	..	..	..
181	Cooks, water carriers, door-keepers, watchmen and other indoor servants.	148	83	6	1	..	57	117	64	7	1	..	46	24	12	1	..	..	11	7	7	..	..	..	..
182	Private grooms, coachmen, dog-boys, etc.	65	49	..	..	..	16	20	5	..	..	..	15	45	44	..	..	..	1	..	..	..	..	..	..
	XI.—INSUFFICIENTLY DESCRIBED OCCUPATIONS.	565	441	11	39	..	113	215	99	9	6	..	107	347	339	2	33	..	6	3	3	..	..	..	..
	53.—General terms which do not indicate a definite occupation.	565	441	11	39	..	113	215	99	9	6	..	107	347	339	2	33	..	6	3	3	..	..	..	..
184	Manufacturers, business-men and contractors otherwise unspecified.	27	2	2	..	..	23	22	2	..	..	..	20	5	..	2	..	..	3	..	..	..	..	..	..
185	Cashiers, accountants, book-keepers, clerks, and other employés in unspecified offices, warehouses and shops.	77	22	5	1	..	50	69	17	5	1	..	47	6	3	..	..	..	3	2	2	..	..	..	..
186	Mechanics otherwise unspecified.	3	..	..	..	..	3	3	..	..	..	..	3	..	..	..	..	..	..	..	..	..	..	..	..
187	Labourers and workmen otherwise unspecified.	458	417	4	38	..	37	121	80	4	5	..	37	336	336	..	33	..	..	1	1	..	..	..	..
	XII.—UNPRODUCTIVE .	11,525	11,107	368	..	..	50	11,383	10,969	364	..	..	50	95	91	4	..	..	..	47	47	..	..	..	..
	54.—Inmates of jails, asylums and almshouses.	11,512	11,098	367	..	..	47	11,370	10,960	363	..	..	47	95	91	4	..	..	..	47	47	..	..	..	..
188	Inmates of jails, asylums and almshouses.	11,512	11,098	367	..	..	47	11,370	10,960	363	..	..	47	95	91	4	..	..	..	47	47	..	..	..	..
	55.—Beggars, vagrants, prostitutes.	13	9	1	..	..	3	13	9	1	..	..	3	..	..	..	..	..	..	..	..	..	..	..	..
189	Beggars, vagrants, witches, wizards, etc.	13	9	1	..	..	3	13	9	1	..	..	3	..	..	..	..	..	..	..	..	..	..	..	..

Table XX.—Distribution by Religion of Workers and Dependants in different Occupations.

Note.—The estimated Andamanese (577) and Nicobarese (375) are omitted from this Table.

Occupation and Group Number.	Total workers and dependants.	Distribution by Religion.							
		Hindu.	Arya.	Sikh.	Buddhist.	Musalman.	Christian.	Animist.	Confucian.
1	2	3	4	5	6	7	8	9	10
Andamans and Nicobars	**26,134**	**8,814**	**66**	**390**	**2,652**	**4,104**	**1,586**	**8,222**	**300**
1. Income from rent of agricultural land	159	3	1	..	..	..	155	..	..
2. Ordinary Cultivators	9,668	1,322	21	7	24	284	358	7,652	..
3. Agents, clerks, managers of landed estates	8	..	..	..	..	7	1	..	..
7. Fruit, betel, vegetable, vine, etc., growers	588	20	..	..	..	..	7	561	..
8. Forest officers, rangers, guards, etc.	350	28	..	..	2	..	320	..	..
9. Wood cutters; firewood, catechu, rubber, etc., collectors and charcoal burners.	6	6	..	..	..	..	..	..	..
14. Herdsmen, shepherds, goatherds, etc.	14	13	..	..	..	1	..	..	..
15. Birds, bees, etc.	1	1	..	..	..	..	..	..	..
17. Fishing	7	7	..	..	..	..	..	..	..
27. Cotton sizing and weaving	17	7	..	..	..	10	..	..	..
43. Sawyers	29	10	..	..	18	1	..	..	..
44. Carpenters, turners and joiners, etc.	55	5	..	..	3	3	44	..	..
45. Basket makers and other industries of woody material, including leaves and thatchers and builders working with bamboo reeds or similar materials.	15	..	..	..	5	10	..	..	..
65. Rice pounders and huskers and flour grinders	7	..	..	..	..	7	..	..	..
66. Bakers and biscuit makers	11	11	..	..	..	..	..	..	..
67. Grain parchers, etc.	5	3	..	..	..	..	2	..	..
74. Toddy drawers	3	..	..	..	..	3	..	..	..
77. Tailors, milliners, dress makers, darners and embroiderers on linen.	21	10	..	..	1	9	1	..	..
78. Shoe, boot and sandal makers	3	3	..	..	..	..	..	..	..
80. Washing, cleaning and dyeing	4	3	..	..	..	1	..	..	..
81. Barbers, hair dressers and wig makers	11	10	..	..	..	1	..	..	..
93. Gas works and electric light and power	2	..	..	..	..	2	..	..	..
94. Printers, lithographers, engravers, etc.	2	2	..	..	..	..	..	..	..
98. Workers in precious stones and metals, enamellers, imitation jewellery makers, gilders, etc.	23	14	..	..	..	9	..	..	..
101. Others, including managers, persons (other than performers) employed in theatres and other places of public entertainment, employés of public societies, etc.	2	..	..	..	..	2	..	..	..
103. Sweepers, scavangers, etc.	13	6	..	..	..	7	..	..	..
105. Persons (other than labourers) employéd in harbours and docks including pilots.	8	8	..	..	..	..	..	..	..
107. Ship owners and their employés, shipbrokers, ships officers, engineers, mariners and firemen.	85	11	..	..	..	..	..	..	74
114. Cart drivers and owners	4	3	..	..	1	..	..	..	..
117. Porters and messengers	12	5	..	..	..	5	2	..	..
118. Railway employés of all kinds other than coolies	34	8	..	..	1	17	8	..	..
120. Post office, Telegraph and Telephone services	32	..	..	..	..	20	12	..	..
121. Bank managers, money lenders, exchange and insurance agents, money changers and brokers and their employés.	2	..	..	..	..	..	2	..	..
122. Brokers, commission agents, commercial travellers, warehouse owners and employés.	9	..	..	..	9	..	..	..	..
128. Trade in chemical products (drugs, dyes, paints, petroleum, explosives, etc.).	17	17	..	..	..	..	..	..	..
132. Grocers and sellers of vegetable oil, salt and other condiments	14	14	..	..	..	..	..	..	..
133. Sellers of milk, butter, ghee, etc.	65	55	..	..	..	10	..	..	..
134. Sellers of sweetmeats, sugar, gur and molasses	30	28	..	1	..	..	1	..	..
135. Cardamom, betel-leaf, vegetables, fruit and areca nut sellers	253	9	..	..	4	20	..	5	215
136. Grain and pulse dealers	9	9	..	..	..	..	..	..	..
140. Trade in ready made clothing and other articles of dress, etc.	53	46	..	..	..	6	1	..	..
152. General storekeepers and shopkeepers otherwise unspecified	307	61	..	..	47	191	4	4	..
155. Army (Imperial)	672	180	..	4	..	391	97	..	..
157. Navy	2	..	..	2	..	..	..	..	..
159. Police	283	89	6	183	..	1	4	..	..
160. Village watchmen	48	39	..	..	..	3	6	..	..
161. Service of the State	546	308	..	4	30	183	21	..	..
164. Village officials and servants other than watchmen	3	..	..	3	..	..	..	..	..
165. Priests, ministers, etc.	2	..	..	..	..	..	2	..	..
166. Religious mendicants, inmates of monasteries, etc.	32	11	..	..	7	..	14	..	..
170. Lawyers' clerks, petition writers, etc.	3	..	..	..	..	3	..	..	..
171. Medical practitioners of all kinds, including dentists, oculists and veterinary surgeons.	192	..	..	178	10	..	4	..	..
172. Midwives, vaccinators, compounders, nurses, masseurs, etc.	32	32	..	..	..	..	..	..	..
173. Professors and teachers of all kinds	10	..	..	..	..	9	1	..	..
174. Clerks and servants connected with education	14	14	..	..	..	..	..	..	..
176. Architects, surveyors, engineers, and their employés	17	..	..	..	..	3	14	..	..
180. Proprietors (other than of agricultural land), fund and scholarship holders and pensioners.	17	1	..	1	..	9	6	..	..
181. Cooks, water carriers, doorkeepers, watchmen and other indoor servants.	148	50	..	..	..	50	48	..	..
182. Private grooms, coachmen, dog boys, etc.	65	6	..	..	..	1	58	..	..
184. Manufacturers, business men and contractors otherwise unspecified.	27	24	..	..	2	..	1	..	..
185. Cashiers, accountants, book-keepers, clerks, and other employés in unspecified offices, warehouses and shops.	77	22	..	1	15	33	6	..	..
186. Mechanics otherwise unspecified	3	..	..	..	3	..	..	..	..
187. Labourers and workmen otherwise unspecified	458	96	..	..	19	13	330	..	..
188. Inmates of jails, asylums and almshouses	11,512	6,177	38	5	2,451	2,774	56	..	11
189. Beggers, vagrants, witches wizards, etc.	13	7	..	1	..	5	..	..	..

SUPPLEMENTARY TABLE.

Population of Local Areas by Sex and Religion.

Name of Circle.	Occupied houses.	Population.			Hindu. (Brahmanic).		Arya.		Sikh.		Buddhist.		Musalman.		Christian.		Animist.		Confucian.	
		Persons.	Males.	Females.	Males.	Females.	Males.	Females.	Males.	Females.	Males.	Females.	Males.	Females.	Males.	Females.	Males.	Females.	Males.	Females.
1	2	3	4	5	6	7	8	9	10	11	12	13	14	15	16	17	18	19	20	21
Andamans and Nicobars	**3,310**	**27,086**	**20,793**	**6,293**	**7,455**	**1,359**	**65**	**1**	**366**	**24**	**2,580**	**72**	**3,650**	**454**	**1,461**	**125**	**4,917**	**4,257**	**299**	**1**
Port Blair	**1,562**	**15,675**	**13,747**	**1,928**	**7,267**	**1,332**	**65**	**1**	**363**	**24**	**2,361**	**44**	**3,394**	**446**	**297**	**81**	..	..	..	..
Circle 1	351	4,155	3,528	627	1,936	392	4	..	37	3	634	4	837	177	80	51	..	..	..	..
" 2	16	1,727	1,485	242	834	200	6	..	47	3	278	8	312	29	8	2	..	..	..	..
" 3	479	4,435	3,663	772	2,005	595	22	1	69	6	609	28	911	130	47	12	..	..	..	..
" 4	337	2,237	2,135	102	1,165	81	25	..	29	..	363	4	522	14	31	3	..	..	..	..
" 5	289	2,143	2,058	85	1,099	50	8	..	25	2	388	..	518	28	20	5	..	..	..	..
Cantonment	90	978	878	100	228	14	..	..	156	10	89	..	294	68	111	8	..	..	..	..
Rest of Andamans	**172**	**2,139**	**1,804**	**335**	**182**	**27**	..	..	..	..	**118**	**14**	**67**	**7**	**1,127**	**20**	**310**	**267**	..	..
North Andaman	145	1,143	1,080	63	172	27	..	..	..	..	101	14	65	7	742	15	..	..	..	..
Middle "	27	419	414	5	10	..	..	..	..	..	17	..	2	..	385	5	..	..	..	..
Jarawa*	..	231	106	125	..	..	..	..	..	..	..	..	..	..	..	..	106	125	..	..
Onge*	..	346	204	142	..	..	..	..	..	..	..	..	..	..	..	..	204	142	..	..
Nicobars	**1,576**	**9,272**	**5,242**	**4,030**	**6**	..	..	..	**3**	..	**101**	**14**	**189**	**1**	**37**	**24**	**4,607**	**3,990**	**299**	**1**
Car Nicobar	1,098	6,364	3,522	2,842	2	..	..	..	3	..	68	14	185	1	37	24	3,227	2,803	..	..
Chowra	82	234	141	93	..	..	..	..	..	..	..	..	..	..	..	..	141	93	..	..
Teressa	129	596	328	268	..	..	..	..	..	..	..	..	..	..	..	..	282	268	46	..
Bompoka	18	83	43	40	..	..	..	..	..	..	..	..	..	..	..	..	42	40	1	..
Camorta	93	575	338	237	4	..	..	..	..	..	..	..	3	..	..	..	309	237	22	..
Nancowry	29	172	94	78	..	..	..	..	..	..	..	..	1	..	..	..	87	78	6	..
Trinkot	18	68	38	30	..	..	..	..	..	..	..	..	..	..	..	..	32	30	6	..
Great Nicobar	13	85	41	44	..	..	..	..	..	..	..	..	..	..	..	..	41	44	..	..
Little Nicobar	7	33	12	21	..	..	..	..	..	..	..	..	..	..	..	..	12	21	..	..
Pulo Milo	3	31	16	15	..	..	..	..	..	..	..	..	..	..	..	..	12	14	..	1
Kondul	6	72	30	42	..	..	..	..	..	..	..	..	..	..	..	..	30	42	..	..
Katchall	80	341	206	135	..	..	..	..	..	..	..	..	..	..	..	..	164	135	42	..
Trading vessel	..	243	243	..	..	..	..	..	..	..	33	..	..	..	..	..	38	..	172	..
Shom Pen*	..	375	190	185	..	..	..	..	..	..	..	..	..	..	..	..	190	185	..	..

* Estimated population for which no schedules were prepared.